**Community Care
Practice Handbooks**

General Editor: Martin Davies

Adolescents and Social Workers

**Community Care
Practice Handbooks**

General Editor: Martin Davies

Adolescents and Social Workers

Margaret Crompton

HEINEMANN EDUCATIONAL BOOKS
LONDON

TO
DORNA, JO, PETER,
AND JOHN

Heinemann Educational Books Ltd
22 Bedford Square, London WC1B 3HH
LONDON   EDINBURGH   MELBOURNE   AUCKLAND
HONG KONG   SINGAPORE   KUALA LUMPUR   NEW DELHI
IBADAN   NAIROBI   JOHANNESBURG
EXETER (NH)   KINGSTON   PORT OF SPAIN

British Library Cataloguing in Publication Data

Crompton, Margaret

    Adolescents and social workers. — (Community care practice handbooks; 12)
    1. Social work with youth — Great Britain
    2. Interpersonal relations
    I. Title II. Series
    362.7'96'0941   HV1441.G7
    ISBN 0-435-82189-X

Typeset by Inforum Ltd, Portsmouth, and printed by Biddles Ltd, Guildford, Surrey.

Contents

Foreword

A social worker friend responded to a question about how to work with adolescents that it was all 'about treating adolescents like other human beings'. 'Today', wrote his wife, 'he recounted that he had screamed at the Universe, Life and the World in general about the impossibility of work with difficult 15-year-olds.'

This book is about the possibility of treating difficult 15-year-olds like other human beings!

Acknowledgements
I have received a great deal of help from friends and colleagues employed in social work and elsewhere who have talked, written, and sent articles to me. Some are mentioned in the text and to all I offer my deepest gratitude for time, ideas and encouragement. I can mention by name, here, only four individuals: Dorna, Peter and Jo who as adolescents treated me like another human being and gave all they could to this book to try to help other adolescents: and John Crompton whose faith, patience and typing ensured that the book left my head and reached the publisher. And I particularly wish to thank the staff of the Brian Stanley Library of the University of Newcastle.

I am grateful to the Northorpe Hall Trust for the cover illustration.

Notes
I have made no attempt to differentiate between England and Wales, Scotland, and Northern Ireland, where some legal and administrative details in social work practice vary.

Where generalisations are used, social workers are referred to as 'she' and adolescents are referred to as 'he'.

1 'The Vitality of the Young People Themselves'*

Introduction

When I first planned this book I thought it would be interesting to devote a short last chapter to the ideas and comments of some adolescents speaking for themselves. I had some doubts about this for I did not want simply to reproduce already printed material. Some months later I sat down to write, knowing that my possible little endpiece would instead be the first, and possibly the most important, chapter. I owe this to three remarkable people who have written for and/or talked with me about their experience of being adolescent and, in particular, of contact with professional adult helpers. I have been honoured by their confidence and stimulated by their interest in using this book to try to help others. Nothing in this chapter appears without their permission.

Dorna

Dorna has asked to remain anonymous and chose her pseudonym herself. All names in her contributions are also disguised.

As I write she is 16, has been in care since the age of three months and is now living in a foster home. She is engaged to a young man whom she has known for many years but does not plan to marry immediately. She has a Youth Opportunities job which provides her with a great deal of responsibility and which she enjoys.

Dorna was introduced to me by her social worker because she had been compiling a file on various projects and topics including glue-sniffing, drugs and alcohol, using both the experiences of her friends and written information. Up to the date of writing this we have met several times, meetings when I have enjoyed Dorna's company and unfailingly interesting conversation and have learned more than from any book or course. Dorna herself has written two long pieces for this chapter and has collected specially written comments on social work from a number of her friends.

Jo

I have known Jo for some years, first meeting her when, as a friend of her parents, I watched from afar as she struggled through a very

* Robinson 1981

painful crisis at 15. Using her formidable will-power she later passed, though suffering terrible anxiety, a long list of GCE 'O' levels and is now preparing to take 'A' levels and applying for a place at a teacher training college. She is clear and sensible about her own plans, and passionate and energetic in the cause of peace and disarmament.

Her contribution to this book comes partly from notes written after a long fireside conversation and a subsequent letter, but is also from my memory of her through our developing friendship, helping my understanding of and thoughts about 'adolescence'.

Peter

Peter was introduced to me by a mutual friend with whom he had a temporary home. All his homes are temporary. He bravely agreed to talk to me and gave me two hours which cost him no little distress, for raking over the past pains cannot be done without cost – and Peter's pains are by no means all in the past. His confusing life in and out of special schools and children's homes has led him at 19 to be in a remand centre awaiting trial on various charges.

Peter is hardly literate (in letters he expresses himself vividly but in unorthodox spelling) and his comments recorded in this chapter are taken from semi-verbatim records which I made during and after our talk. This talk was, at his suggestion, conducted in a rather straight interview way, that is I asked questions and he replied in rather jerky phrases and sentences, until he dried up and I questioned again.

Unlike Dorna, who plans to work in a drugs unit, and Jo, who hopes to train as a teacher, Peter has no clear plan. Unlike Jo, he refused to sign a petition for nuclear disarmament. Dorna took a copy of the petition to get further signatures. I stress just for a moment the dissimilarities between my three friends because the most important impression I have is their likeness one to another – not in appearance or background or even experience, but in beauty and intelligence, the ability to be in touch with themselves and to communicate this. I have written of them as 'remarkable' and in any group of people they would be outstanding. They certainly command my especial respect. But I believe that what they have to say and to give may be found in many people, less articulate but with as much understanding as Jo, as much love as Dorna, as much pain as Peter. For those who have ears to hear and who care enough to listen, there are many voices.

'Inside'

Love for one lass

Dorna spent some time in a Community Home with Education on the Premises (CHE), sampling the secure unit and then the 'house'. Here she writes of her life, of the care shown to glue-sniffing Gemma, and of how five girls made 40 others feel love for one, Karen.

The difference between the two units was the freedom. In the secure unit the rules were very strict and done to the minute. I mean tea was always at five o'clock, clear up at quarter to six. Lock up till seven then television (or records) for two hours, at nine showers, nine fifteen supper, dishes done by nine thirty, then bed; lights out by ten. Day after day same thing to the minute. On every window either bars or locks. Smoking was a privilege which had to be earned. I found myself rocking the time away (or making up poems). The more rules you have the more you want to break them. Beat the system so to speak. If you absconded you were looked upon as God. For some reason. To be out for just five minutes was paradise.

All the lasses in the secure unit were there for a reason. Obviously for breaking the law. Every one of them tried to beat the system. Out of 12 lasses six were chosen for the 'house'. The worst ones. I was one of the six along with Gemma, Karen, Patty, Maralyn and Judy. All of us were absconders and were classed as uncontrollable. When we moved to the 'house' what a change it made.

The house was out of the grounds of the actual home and there were very few rules. No bars on windows and we did all our own cooking. *We were made to feel like human beings not animals*. Because of this we all felt we owed something to our Gaffer so we abided by the rules. We did them of our own free will. Never once were we ordered to do something. And because of this we didn't mind doing it. If you did break the rules you weren't punished with force you were punished with your own guilt and whatever the lasses thought should happen to you.

I'll give you one example. Gemma was heavy into glue. One night she went out and came back stotting, [dead 'drunk']. Sheila said nowt to her except 'are you alright Gemma, can I get you anything?' It's not that she didn't care, she did, but she didn't want to play the heavy hand. So when Gemma came through the sitting room sulking 'cos of lack of attention we showed her how much we cared by kicking her all over. This wasn't done out of spite. We all loved her and the only way to make her feel wanted was to do this and show just how much we did care. Gemma never took glue again after that night and to think she'd been on it for a year and a half! All it took was a bit of love to get her off it. So you see, Gemma was punished and her punishment gave her back her sense and self-respect.

Another incident which occurred was with Karen. She'd gone home on leave and while at home stole some lead off a swimming pool roof. All the lasses had a discussion and we decided her punishment should be to ignore her so she knew we were all disappointed in her. She'd ruined any clean report and no way was she going to get away with it. Karen came back to a morgue. Even at table when she asked for stuff nobody took any notice. She started to feel her guilt and she was very sorry for what she'd done. When we all thought she'd had her punishment Karen talked about it with the rest of us and we found out more about her problems. So we decided to put them right for her. Eventually she was sorted out.

The day she went to a court a letter off the 'house' lasses went with her. A letter to say we would all vouch for Karen if she did anything wrong again. Sort of like being on bail. We all wrote what we felt, *a kind of love which you only experience in a home*. Karen was made to feel more than she had ever been in her life. Five lasses she'd only met three months before were prepared to stake their lives for her. Karen was choked and the happiest girl on this earth. What was said in that letter was meant and felt. The morning she went an awful silence fell over the entire place. *Five lasses made 40 others feel this love for one lass*. Meadowgrove was like a graveyard. Nobody in the 'house' ate all day and our minds and hearts were with Karen. To experience this was unbelievable because it seemed to catch on to the staff. The silence was almost unbearable; it was as if the whole place was going to erupt any minute. We were all just waiting for Karen to return. Her family and social worker had no faith in her at all but the 'house' lasses were with her all the way.

I'll never forget the instant change of atmosphere when Karen walked through the classroom door. The textbooks, rulers, pens, all the arms and cheers went up. Karen's face beamed all over. I rushed over to meet her and the tears of joy streamed down her face. From that day on Karen was a changed lass, she's back in society and the guilt has been dropped. The chip on her shoulder fell off and the first words she spoke were 'If ever I see a lass in care go the way I have I can help her just like you've helped me'. [My italics]

The size of problem everyone can handle

Dorna wrote with the same practically focused love that she showed in her treatment of Gemma. She hoped to reach, through social workers and other caring adults, other Gemmas. Once she found a young boy in a field, just beginning his first-ever sniff. She stopped him, briskly, took him home with her, gave him tea and told him, with the aid of posters, the dangers of his behaviour. Hours later the boy left, safe, at least for the time being. Dorna's confidence in writing and intervening has grown 'because I've lived with and seen a lot of my friends go through the stages of glue and I believe with a bit more help and understanding from you lot out there this *Big* problem will turn into the size of problem everyone can handle'. This is, surely, true of many problems.

Glue is supposed to be an adhesive, but these days a lot of young kids use it to sniff. Most of them do it because of boredom. Others do it to rid themselves of their problems and to make themselves feel happy. It makes you forget your bad memories and situations at the time in which you sniff but afterwards they're still there.

Everyone sees different hallucinations. One girl saw a little man in her glue bag and table legs looked like snakes. She talked to people that weren't there. Another girl saw witches and moving graves. Another saw her pop idol. She also saw herself dying; she explained 'I am going up a black tube with forget-me-nots in the wall. I am on my way to heaven.' She also sees herself as a witch and the glue bag as a bomb. She continued 'My friend and I are in prison, this is one hallucination I'm always having.' That is where she will probably end up.

Think about your families, your mates and the people who are worse off than yourselves, and there *Are* such people. Or is it that you don't want to face reality? Maybe you're frightened because your friends will reject you. These people aren't your friends – they're your murderers.

(Wilson, D. 1981; see also pp. 28–9)

On social workers

Becoming a successful social worker

David has not been at the receiving end of social work help. These views on social work are taken from writing about his plans to become a social worker.

To be a good social worker you have to be a good listener with a sympathetic nature and most of all you have to know how to advise the kids in the best way fit. I think I would be a good social worker especially with teenagers as I would be able to understand their problems much better than the adults of today.

I think what really got me interested in being a social worker was doing humanities at school. Humanities is like a sociology lesson but does not have such a wide span and keeps it pretty simple. So far my own experience with children was at the playschool. The playschool is part of the practical side of the humanities lesson. I liked working with the kids as it was good experience for me. The age varied from six months to five years. Our main task was to keep the kids amused the best way we could. This proved to be harder than it sounds and involved a lot of time and thought.

I know a couple of kids in care and they don't seem to mind it. Either they enjoy it or they think they're better off in care anyway. They told me that they like their social workers and they were easy to get on with. I do however know this is not always the case.

Some people I have talked to say being a social worker is not the best job in the world, because you have a lot of pressure on you and such a lot of people rely on your judgement. I realise the job involves a lot of emotional stress and it can lead to unsocial hours but I am sure I will be able to cope with all these minor disadvantages.

Pack up and do another decent job

Alan writes from experience in care and borstal.

Social workers should be there when they are needed not just when you are in trouble. If you do happen to be in trouble with the law they should try to help you not squeak on you. In other words when they know you nicked something they should just keep quiet and let the police do their job without any help from the social worker. I have no time at all for my social worker because she's too damn nosey about things which don't concern her at all. My social worker thinks she knows me but she doesn't. How could she? I hardly see her. She makes me feel like a kid at school. I mean she always pulls her rank on me. I don't care if she's the Queen, I still wouldn't tell her nowt. The message I give to social workers is pack up and do another decent job. If they want to help people they should work with spastics or old people.

It takes the real thing, not study
Josie now lives in a flat.

When you need money for college books and clothes etc., they should be able to supply it. They say they're there to help – well, these things are needed and they could help by giving you some cash to get them. They don't gain your trust and respect because they are too inquisitive. They shouldn't ask questions – they should wait until you're ready to tell them. Instead of palming you off in different homes they do a foster review. I mean they should get to know you and shop around and see what home you would be suited in. Then send you there to make a life for yourself. It would save a lot of time and money if they thought a bit more about this suggestion.

To train them the best way would be to put them in a home as staff without any responsibilities, kind of like the kid himself. *You can't learn kids through books*. It takes the real thing, not study. I know; I'm at college and it's just the basics you learn.   [my italics]

A bloody hard job
Sandra too lives in a flat.

I think a social worker is a person not an animal like some people think they are. A social worker is somebody who tries to help you with your problems. A lot of the time they try to avoid you. But when they come to see you they don't seem to do anything, just talk. In fact *they get paid for the patter not the action*.

I have now been in care a number of years. I have been helped by social workers. But most of the time I have had to do it myself and when they do try to help, they go about it the wrong way and all they do is annoy me. They are always there when you don't want them or need them and when you do need them they are hard to find.

I don't trust my social worker one little bit as everything I say goes in her little black book. The trouble with social workers is there isn't enough of them. There are too many kids to one social worker and they have too many problems to sort out. Not even a wife and husband can sort out their own so how in hell are they supposed to sort out 40 kids' problems and see them once a week? It's impossible.

The message I give to people who want to be social workers is good luck to them because they've got a bloody hard job and don't be frightened to get involved with the kids 'cos *the more involved you are the more they respect you*. Also give them a lot of love and attention and they'll tell you all you want to know (all their problems). [my italics]

Sandra's mistrust of her social worker derived from incidents such as this: when at one time she was in need of accommodation, the social worker suggested that she should take the contraceptive pill. Sandra and her friends were very offended for they thought this advice implied a grave insult. Sandra felt that she was expected to become sexually available, possibly to anyone who offered a bed. She felt that her social worker had failed to understand that she is a person who uses great discrimination in her choice of sexual partners and was in no way a girl who would 'indulge' in intercourse just because she was without a proper home.

What they can blackmail you with later on
Pam is now out of care and has her own child.

> Social workers come and see you once in a blue moon and expect you to tell them all there is to know about you. They say they have to know but half of what you say isn't used, they just want it to see what they can blackmail you with later on.
> I mean, I told my social worker once about my dad bashing me. He had a reason (a good one) and I told her that as well. You know what she did? She stopped my weekends, said it was due to circumstances at home. She just didn't like to see me happy so she did this.

Numbers not kids
Mark is now out of borstal and settled in a flat and work.

> I think social workers look upon you as numbers not kids. I mean you're filed under section not name. They should be able to knock some sense into you so you wouldn't end up in borstals and detention centres or places like this. If they could also knock sense into waggers [truants] from school they wouldn't end up being unhappy in children's homes; they would still be at home with the security of their parents. If more social workers took more time with your problems, not just half an hour once a month, more kids would be settled down in families and not in children's homes or borstals.
> When you think about it your social worker is a kind of habit. He just comes when you're in trouble. *When you're good nobody remembers but when you're bad nobody forgets.* Social workers will never understand young kids so I would tell them just to pack up and go home to their family and be thankful they've got somebody who loves them. [my italics]

If you had more responsibility you'd have more respect – Peter
The good: In his early teens Peter spent some time in a residential special school for bright maladjusted children. He was happy there – 'really good'. He described the headmistress as 'a lovely lady – attractive – intelligent –*she cared not just because she was meant to – she did care'.* Together with her husband, also resident at the school,

Peter saw her as 'the perfect mother and father – and dog'. He preferred to stay in the school at weekends to going home to his own parents. 'Felt safe there – got self-respect back.'

Later in a children's home he made a good relationship with his assigned careworker. 'Trusted her very much – she was on the level with everything. Pretty new to the game herself – she was learning as well – we helped each other'. [How? I asked] 'Making her laugh – making her enjoy work. Had a lot of sympathy with her – confidential talks about everything – she told me about herself – on the level – showed her emotions'. As the careworker lived in a part of the city well known to Peter, he quite often met her in pubs when she was off duty with friends, and also went to her flat. This helped Peter to see her as a real person. The other people with whom Peter could talk in the home were three careworkers and one cleaning lady.

Feeling like a whole person and not a case is important to Peter. This is what he said about his probation officer: 'At first I couldn't stand him. I was going to stab him.' The social worker had apparently transferred Peter to the probation officer without really explaining why. Peter felt completely rejected by the social worker because he'd 'have to start opening up all over again. However this probation officer is a good bloke – trust him – don't get treated like a client – he thinks I'm a great bloke – I give him advice on photography and other clients.' [Peter later asked me to show this section to the probation officer.]

The bad: As already indicated, Peter did not have a very good opinion of his field social worker. In the home, the fieldworker visited at first weekly, then fortnightly, 'sorting out problems – talking to careworkers – general assessment'. Occasionally Peter and the careworkers saw the fieldworker together; he hated the fieldworker and careworkers talking together without him and also hated them keeping files he couldn't see. 'Social worker said it was part of his job – *you just felt 'client' full stop – felt like an object*.' Peter broke in and saw his file – 'Got to me too much – very boring – you knew all the bad things – you wondered what they thought of you – a lot of bad reports' [Did they write good things too? I asked] 'and good reports.' [I asked Peter if he would like to fill in his own file; he said no, but he wouldn't mind so much if he could see what was written.] Peter 'trusted social worker at first – I needed help and the only way to get it is to tell them. Lost trust because talked to careworkers.' Peter had thought that everything he said to the fieldworker was in confidence.

With the exception of the people already mentioned Peter regarded the care staff as 'the Gestapo – you didn't talk to them – I didn't know what they were offering – everything by the book – no give either way – no guidance – thought we'd respect them more because they were authority figures – "you do it because I'm right and I say so" – everyone says I'm useless – what he says must be right – so you feel more inadequate'.

Peter has been feeling useless and inadequate since he was five. No wonder he is angry when the professional helpers only seem to reinforce this; and thank goodness he has met a few at least who have regarded him as the whole, real person he is. Speaking of his idea of being an adult he said: 'want to go out and have fun – but if you had more responsibility you'd have more respect'.

[My italics]

Finding out the hard way – Dorna

Social workers never gain your trust mainly because they are classed as a voice of authority.

The first lesson you're taught when you move into a children's home is *never* to trust your social worker. This has a lot to do with it. I mean when ten or 11 kids are saying this to you you don't forget it easily. Respect is a word never used about social workers. Respect is for your mates. It sounds silly but a social worker is a kind of bad omen to kids in care. Someone who's there when not needed. Someone who knows practically everything there is to know about you. Someone who reads reports by other voices in authority and what is said on file paper – it *must* for some unknown reason be the real you.

They don't stop to think for one minute you might not have liked the place you were at so you worked yourself rotten to get out of it. Eventually you did get out but with a black cloud hung over your head and a piece of paper saying 'Beware, this child is violently aggressive'. This is what annoys me hot about social workers. If they never looked at your files and decided to find out for themselves what you're really like it would save a lot of hard feelings. To be able to say to your kid: 'Listen, I've never read your file so it's up to you to what you tell me!' They would get a lot further on. Some social workers already use this line but they forget every kid knows they have to read their files before they've even met them. If it was true and they hadn't read their files that's where the trust and respect starts.

Social workers forget to think what it would be like if that particular child knew their life story – how would they feel towards them? I mean if it was compulsory that when you became a social worker your kids had to know all about you.

Social workers behave towards kids as a kind of police man. They're looked upon as a screw. They also make you feel a total idiot. I mean they'll say to you 'Well how is such and such?' You know they already know so you say 'What you asking me for, you already know.' They usually reply 'But I want to hear off you.' Now what is the sense of that? The only thing they want is to be able to say to their bosses 'Fred told me all about the incident in his own words.' All of a sudden they think they've got you where they want you. People only tell them what they don't mind anyone else knowing. The kids only tell them as much as they want them to know, nothing else.

A social worker shouldn't be like anything, they should just be themselves. Forget all they've learnt out of books, forget all the boring lectures and get down to some real work. They shouldn't go to college and all that kind of stuff because it's a complete waste of time. Life doesn't come in books.

The rummaging psychiatrist

(This is not a hit at psychiatrists; Jo's experiences could have been repeated with social workers, teachers, psychologists – any 'helping professionals'.)

When Jo was 15 everything happened at once: her grandfather died, her father had a minor but worrying operation, she entered her 'O' level year and her mother became pregnant. Jo 'began to feel very unhappy without really knowing why'; she 'became obsessional about eating', rationed her food and exercised. She was already twig-slim and now slipped perilously near to a state of *anorexia nervosa*. Jo and her parents accepted referral to a child psychiatric unit where Jo saw a psychiatrist – and was not impressed, although she, perhaps generously, thinks that he may have helped her if only by default.

The psychiatrist's first mistake was a failure in courtesy. He sat with his feet on the desk and smoked 'to put me at my ease'. But the putting-at-ease does not seem to have extended very far. Jo loathes cigarette smoke but although he did ask if she minded, 'because it was about the first thing he said to me, I didn't feel I could say "Yes, please don't." It was obviously his room, and who was I to stop him smoking?' And while she was 'Joanna' he was firmly 'Dr X'. (Why not 'Joanna' and 'Albert', 'Jo and 'Bert' or 'Miss A' and 'Dr X'?) Jo's feet were not invited onto the desk top!

Jo felt that Dr X was trying to 'slot me into a pigeon-hole', that he had a model of adolescent girls which she did not fit. Not fitting seemed to imply that she was 'odd'. For example, she did not have 'strings of boyfriends', or like discos, and she did talk freely to her parents; all, apparently, highly unusual in teenage girls. Jo felt that all would have been well for Dr X if she had confessed to repressing anger or being jealous of her pregnant mother:

My food problems and so on started before Mummy even conceived Thomas. Then, when I was referred to Dr X the [unit] lost my referral card. By the time my second referral card was processed and I got to see Dr X I was already on the up because by this time Mummy had conceived Thomas. That is, time scale = (1) beginning of problem; (2) Mummy conceived Thomas; (3) first referral to Dr X; (4) first referral card lost; (5) second referral card to Dr X; (6) I began to get better; (7) first visit to Dr X. Dr X never cottoned onto this, and saw the scale as being 2, 1, 3, 4, 5, 7, 6!

Jo found Dr X's comments about her upbringing critical and insulting to herself and her family. And she felt that he was 'rummaging around inside me to find a me I didn't want to find' – not from fear of finding an unacceptable 'me' but because the psychiatrist seemed to be trying to impose characteristics which Jo did not possess.

But there were things which Dr X could have given Jo. For what she really wanted was 'reassurance', to know that she was normal – not in a pigeon-hole or replica way but as an unique person having normal, ordinary experiences. She could talk to her parents in absolute trust and freedom but at this time she would have liked reassurance from someone detached from the family, perhaps unbiased because not related. Jo had few friends of her own age, her best friend being in London, 300 miles away. She did confide in one school friend but this stopped when she discovered that her confidences had been 'betrayed'. Far from 'strings of boyfriends', Jo needed a trustworthy local girlfriend or two.

The need for detached reassurance arose from the crisis not, as it was all too easy to assume, of her mother's pregnancy, but of her own position on a precarious ledge between childhood and adulthood.

> At first I regretted having left my very happy childhood. I longed to revert to those days I remembered as worryless, but didn't feel like a child any more. It was only as I began to see the positive things about being an adult – for example, that responsibilities weren't necessarily burdens – that I began to look forward to being an adult. But at both stages (that is, wanting to be a child and second, wanting to be an adult) I hated being where I was – hanging between both types of life where I saw there was happiness and peace of mind.

She saw other things too, for example, that adults have problems and feelings, and she learned about death and birth. Her grandfather's death disturbed her and she was filled with guilt. She told her father that she thought she should have written to him every week. But her father said no, there had been no such need, for her grandfather had had great pleasure watching her grow up. From this she learned, to her amazement, that adults do not love only babies. Jo wrote:

Also at this time my other grandpa was getting weaker and weaker with a wasting disease, but by the time he died (shortly after Thomas's birth) I was strong enough again to cope with it. His decline in its early stages did worry me very much when I was unstable in my mind.

It was in fact Thomas's arrival that showed me that being an adult didn't have to exclude the pleasures of childhood, that is, through watching children play and grow you could get amazing pleasure. Also, his arrival gave me the insight that as well as death there was new life.

As a postscript Jo wrote to me:

A bit of 'by the way': I've just seen a homeopathic doctor *re* the remnants of my weight problem. He is convinced that the reasons for my problems were Grandpa's death and a BCG vaccination that I was given. The latter is a totally new idea, and although he didn't explain why it might have had this effect, I must say that I can believe that these routine injections of chemicals, regardless of the individual receiving the dosage, could have undesired effects. This is not really relevant to your book though!

I think it is highly relevant.

The psychiatrist did help the family in so far as he and his colleagues provided an outlet for the anxiety raised by Jo's behaviour – and clearly there were other sources of anxiety, too. But he seems not to have come anywhere near the real Jo, preferring, I feel, to put an identikit picture on her chair and hoping for a tape to go with it. (For further discussion of labelling see pp. 52–4 below.)

I have not asked Dr X to put his side of the story. The helping adults have plenty of opportunity to talk – too much, according to Jo and Dorna, who both said that 'they should listen more'. It is rare to hear from the other side of the desk: the words and perceptions of Dorna, Jo and Peter are used throughout this book.

2 Ideas of Adolescence

'Have you ever thought of yourself as an adolescent or a teenager?'
'No. I'm a person. I'm skin and bone. I live here. Age is nothing. It's like time, it's nothing. You wouldn't look out in the street and say, "There's adolescent Robert." '

Robert was 18 when he said that, a young man whom I had known through his last years at school and first years in a good job found in a time of high unemployment. He had made an unstressed move from home to a flat and then to another city, not to avoid his family with which his relationship was very happy but to see as much of the world as possible. The long absence of his divorced father and some personal problems in childhood had not prevented him from making clear choices for himself and carrying out his decisions with the full co-operation of his mother, who was loving but not possessive.

In Chapter 1, I introduced the written and spoken comments of several adolescents who had experience of social workers and other professional helpers. Few of them expressed experience of any real understanding, and some felt that they were expected to conform to some stereotype. In this chapter, I examine some sources of social workers' expectations and stereotyping of adolescence and adolescents. The main theme of this book is that it is essential to meet every adolescent (every client, every person) as an individual. Knowing that *this* individual, Jo or Peter, Dorna or Robert, is experiencing some change related to her or his age is essential to understanding her or his *total* experience, but it may too easily be used to diminish the unique quality of that experience; 'calf-love' or 'an adolescent crush' may be used to devalue great intensity of emotion and 'adolescents are moody' to trivialise real depression.

Some questions for social workers
Social workers might find the following questions useful when preparing to work with adolescents (variants could be used in work with any labelled group).

1. What do *I* mean by 'adolescence'?
2. Where do my ideas and attitudes come from?
3. What do I think about my own adolescence? What can I

remember about it? What evidence is there of (a) events (e.g. photographs, other people's comments) and (b) feeling memories (e.g. diaries)? Does my 'present' affect my memories and interpretations of my adolescence?

4. How do I feel about the adolescents I know now, personally or by repute (e.g. own offspring, siblings, clients, friends' children, friends, attenders at same religious centre, residents at nearby borstal)?

It is essential for the social worker to be in touch with her general attitudes and feelings before embarking on particular contacts.

Personal experience

All social workers have experience of at least one adolescence – their own. For some it may be very recent, for some long past (or at least chronologically long past, for some of the experiences associated with adolescence may remain long after the attainment of 'official' adulthood). It may not always be easy to reach back into one's own adolescence or to distinguish how one really felt then from how one now feels about this or that experience (e.g. indulgent, disappointed, irritated).

One way back to the source of today's attitudes may be old writings and diaries. Here are the dramatic events of two weeks in 1954:

> August 21st. *Scout fête*. Go to Westgate. Saw Henry. At first sight thought the guesthouse awful. Went to beach in afternoon, not *too* bad. In evening walked to Margate with Dad. Also watched TV till 10 p.m. Hope M and V had a good time at scout fête . . . Paul wasn't there. Wish I was at Folkestone. No one decent at guesthouse. 22nd. Went to Church. Very long service but quite nice. Miss girls and scouts. Wish I knew where Paul was. Went to Cliftonville in afternoon. Short walk in evening. Guesthouse not *quite* as bad as at first but could be better. Westgate quite nice. Watched TV. Rather homesick (and boyfriend-sick).
> September 1st. [Usual detailed description of day's activities, then] Beginning to enjoy myself. Walk home with Dad and John who is only 16.
> September 4th. Home from Westgate. In morning raining. Sorry to leave John.

The writer (myself) was 13 and the diary extract recalls for me now not only the baldly noted events but the various feelings. I recognise my present self, too, for example how I feel about and handle going away from my home. An entry at 17 shows feelings of great strength also connected with a move:

October 1st. packed bag, bath. hair set. Goodbye to Mr Covey, Mrs Evans [local shopkeepers]. like an April day. still awful apathetic feeling – till said virtual farewell to Granny and Ken [brother] – at last realise what's about to happen, God bless us all roll on Christmas but may Leeds [university] be super. Thank God for my family.

This note on the end of my childhood compares with the comments of Jo at 17 on her feelings at 15. When Jo goes to college at 18 or 19 she will surely pack her own trunk, for she has already made a firm step into adulthood which 17-year-old Margaret would not achieve for many years.

Public images

Attitudes towards adolescence are also influenced by public figures. Adolescents are constantly exposed to public view through news-papers, radio and television. Porteous and Colston (1980) found that:

> Newspapers show little constructive criticism, help or advice to adol-escents, preferring to report the unusual or sensational behaviour of a small minority. Certain issues of great importance to young people are given very scant attention. In particular unemployment is inadequately covered, and attempts to help our younger generation either in this or any other area are lacking. Educational issues are rarely discussed, and home and family relationships are also ignored. So, while the news-papers' comments on young people are neutral on the whole, we can say that they fall down in what they could do to help their younger readers, and to help their older readers to understand, and assist, young people.

They concluded that:

> The image of young people presented by the press could be significantly improved. Many young people are involved in voluntary activities which help others, but they receive very scant attention and coverage. Similarly, the creative activities of young people are grossly under-mentioned.

We seem to be left with football hooligans and muggers (an image of adolescents as violent and frightening), or crazily-clad pop-idols and fans (anti-conventional, unstable and mindless). The image in teen-focused papers is not very flattering either. *Jackie* for 20.10.79 includes: 'Your special A–Z guide to love and romance', 'They didn't want me! (A reader's true experience told in pictures)', and 'I took the coward's way out' (more true experi-ences). There are also features on fashion and personal problems, 'A day in the life of a kennel maid', and cosmetic and sanitary towel advertisements. The picture is of young girls almost completely obsessed with boyfriends, clothes and cosmetics. My 1954 diary shows how obsessed *I* was with boys but there was a lot more to my life, too. *Jackie* seems to ignore the vast range of interests available to even the most boy-mad girl and to encourage total preoccupation with the self.

Theories and models

Another source of influence and one to which professional helpers are particularly exposed is the mass of theoretical writings about adolescence. The problem is to discover just what one does think and believe and to establish what are the theoretical sources of those beliefs. One training course may focus on one or two models beloved of the lecturer; another may introduce students to a variety of theories; a third may regard adolescence as a solely sociological concept. Is the student's attitude towards adolescence determined by the accident of which course she takes?

To illustrate the problem of recognising influences and defining standpoint, the following extracts represent a few of the many strong and often contradictory ideas to which social workers may be exposed or of which they may not be aware:

1. Adolescents always seem to create more problems than their numbers justify. This is common knowledge . . . (Munro 1978, p. vi)
2. Youth has always been a source of envy, nostalgia and lust to its elders, usually involving a projection onto them that they are enjoying a hedonism we were too respectable or myopic to pursue during our own youth . . . This has resulted in the defin-ition of them as a social problem . . . with the adolescent working-class male, especially, being portrayed as a 'folk devil'. (Brake 1980, pp. viii, 1)
3. Adolescence is unique in its process of growth and develop-ment. It is a period in the life cycle characterised by profound biological and psycho-social change. Not only is there the arrival of reproductive maturity and a rapid acceleration of skeletal growth, but these years also see the final steps in the evolution of a separate identity, and in the acquisition of autonomy. These matters are clearly reflected in teen-agers' intense narcissistic preoccupations with biological integrity, heightened conflict over issues of independence, and major concerns about mastery and control. (Hofmann *et al*. 1976, p. xiii)
4. The adolescent as a distinct species is the creation of modern social attitudes and institutions. A creature neither child nor

adult he is a comparatively recent socio-psychological invention, scarcely two centuries old. Distinctive social institutions have been fashioned to accommodate him; psychologically he has been made more or less to fit them, moulded by appropriate rewards and penalties. . . In general our adolescents are older than we think, our treatment of them barbarous and insulting. (Musgrove 1964, pp. 13, 159)

5. The adolescent is expressing his opinions, not his convictions, for convictions can be based only on experience . . . it is more important that he should be sincere than that he should be right.

In the same way, *the adolescent's views should not be taken too seriously* . . . adolescents are only experimenting with ideas and trying to formulate their opinions. (Hadfield 1962, p. 243)

6. The cure for adolescence is the passage of time, a fact that has very little meaning for the adolescent. (Winnicott 1965, p. 84)

7. It is identity which is first disrupted in early adolescence, gradually becomes reintegrated during mid-adolescence, and finally stabilised in late adolescence or early adulthood. (Lowe 1972, pp. 152–3)

8. The development of *self-responsibility* involves transformations within the individual which match . . . changes in social expectation. This is a process which goes on throughout adult life and is not exclusively tied to one period. We should perhaps speak of a process of adolescing rather than adolescence. (Rayner 1971, p. 140)

9. There is no evidence to show that any but a small minority experience a serious identity crisis. In most cases relationships with parents are positive and constructive and young people, by and large, do not reject adult values in favour of those espoused by the peer group. In fact, in most situations peer group values appear to be consistent with those of important adults, rather than in conflict with them. Fears of promiscuity among the young are not born out by the research findings, nor do studies support the belief that the peer group encourages anti-social behaviour, unless other factors are also present. Lastly there is no evidence to suggest that during the adolescent years there is a higher level of psychopathology than at other times. (Coleman 1980, p. 178)

Although in time past I was influenced by, for example, Hadfield and Winnicott (5 and 6 above), readers may in this book recognise attitudes consistent with the views expressed in the extracts from Brake, Musgrove, Rayner and Coleman (2, 4, 8 and 9 above).

Conclusion

I have suggested some sources of influence on the development of attitudes towards, opinions on and feelings about the adolescents whom social workers encounter. Every news item, every book, every encounter itself, constitutes a fresh influence, something new to be absorbed, to stimulate reaction and that very reaction creates response to the next stimulus. Since we are all (and not only adolescents) in a state of constant change, if only by virtue of ageing, attitudes and feelings, however entrenched they may seem, are also changing. Jo, for example, found that talking and writing about her feelings and experiences changed her perceptions of them.

It is of the greatest importance for the social worker to be clear, to recognise where her ideas come from, where she is prejudiced, lazy, afraid, certain, passionate and so on. The material in the rest of this book will be of little use to a social worker who is not willing to discover her own idea of adolescence.

3 Being and Feeling Adolescent

All generalisations (including our own) about kids were false.
(McKeever 1979, p. 16)

This chapter is about some of the problems which may be experienced by people for whom adolescence is a time of difficulty. This is not to suggest that adolescence is inevitably stressful or that the problems associated with it are necessarily different from those of other times of life. I do not see adolescents with troubles as bundles of gloom and delinquency. They are whole individual people and any problems must be seen as only part of the whole person. The chapter is arranged in two sections, *being adolescent* and *feeling adolescent*.

Being adolescent

Expectations and attitudes of society
Chapter 2 presents some influences on attitudes towards adolescents; adolescents are themselves influenced by the attitudes and expectations of 'society'. For example they may be expected to be moody, moony, intense, self-absorbed, vulnerable, over-sensitive . . . or difficult, rebellious, wild, strangely dressed, violent, gang-centred, sexually hyperactive. Society apparently insists that adolescents will provide plenty of cause for concern. They will not conform to the standards of adult society but will, unless subject to firm controls, break laws and violate mores, while conforming to the standards of their own groups and gangs.

It is very difficult for adolescents to escape such expectations, whether at school, at home or through the media. Teachers, parents and journalists are armed with forebodings and tales of troubles. I have already mentioned the work of Porteous and Colston (1980) who found that the press was on the whole more likely to print stories about 'the unusual or sensational behaviour of a small minority' than about adolescents succeeding or being creative, helpful and socially aware.

Geoffrey Pearson (1978) quotes a Marplan survey finding 'that the preoccupation with "violence . . . is to a significant degree a preoccupation of the elderly" ', who are, that suggests, likely to expect unpleasant behaviour from young people. In the radio serial *The Archers* a group of Hells Angels 'invaded' *The Bull*, causing havoc and violence and giving much opportunity for the locals to mutter about the dreadfulness of the young men (who had probably only called for a drink and were if anything responding to the hostility of the locals). They were, of course, 'set up' for the purposes of the plot; and I suggest that adolescents *are* 'set up' and have a hard time disappointing poor expectations (and getting a fair deal from the scriptwriters).

The fictional Hell's Angels in *The Archers* were doomed because they were labelled by 'OK' society as dangerous and unpleasant. Everyone suffers from labelling ('middle-aged', 'working class', 'female', 'Pakistani', and so on) and from the expectations and attitudes of other people, based on the labels. Part of the problem of *being* adolescent is that that is itself a label.

Teenage marriage is expected to break down, teenage mothers are expected to be immature in their relationships with their babies, and frustrated by being tied down. It is not the custom of this country for adolescents to be encouraged to learn about sexuality and reproduction by experience, even though they may be physically excellently prepared to enjoy intercourse and produce healthy babies. If, for example, it were the custom for girls to have babies who were brought up by their grandmothers, the pattern of behaviour and the constraints and expectations would change.

In Great Britain in the 1980s girls are customarily prepared to be mothers, wives, housewives, working women (however much metalwork they learn at school); boys to be working men, householders, husbands, fathers (with or without cookery classes). The preparation for some of these roles may be rather sketchy, the expectations unrealistic, but those expectations have a deep influence.

Independence – or not
Some time between 16 and 19 one major event occurs for everyone – leaving school (unless for reasons of privilege or incapacity they have not attended school). This means freedom from a way of life which will have lasted for at least 11 years. For some young people this freedom may pose problems. Most obvious is the void created by unemployment; but release from tight structure may also be difficult for those entering further and higher education. It is not easy to plan an academic workload when tutors give out long booklists and require a number of assignments to be completed

within a given period, if the student has been used to the discipline of a teacher and set books. Too much independence is hard to manage.

Starting work probably means a change of structures with a balance of independence/servility depending on the individual occupation. But most employed young people are likely to be in a trainee/apprentice or very junior post, free of school rules but subject to the demands of management and working for eight hours or more.

The other main move into independence may be from home. Students may go to other cities and live in hostels, halls of residence, flats and lodgings. Children in care move from Homes to hostels, lodgings and flats. Service men and women go to training camps, nurses to hospital hostels, and so on. But most school-leavers stay at home, probably until they marry, and so develop their lives as near-adults within the family in which they have been babies and children.

The independence of adolescents is constrained by two powerful externals, *law* and *money*.

The legal position of the adolescent is excellently presented in a publication by the National Council for Civil Liberties (NCCL), *First Rights* (Rae *et al.* 1981). As examples of the anomalous position of adolescents, a boy may join the armed forces at 16, a girl at 17 (both with parents' consent) and they may die at the behest of a government for which they may not vote until 18. A boy may have intercourse legally at 14 but girls must wait until 16. Hire purchase agreements may not be made until 18, when reference from building society or bank is needed, yet the earning adolescent may hold building society and bank accounts and must pay national insurance contributions and income tax.

Few adolescents receive sufficient money, whether as earnings, grants, benefits or pocket money, to live independently of their parents or some other subsidy or to develop the self-respect associated with supporting oneself in one's own home.

School pupils are restricted to whatever pocket money their parents give plus possible earnings from, for example, a paper round. Grant-aided students almost certainly need to spend vacations in parental homes for supplementation by vacation work is no longer easy.

Freedom of action and range of choice in many important areas of life are restricted. Apart from the constraints imposed by legal and financial considerations, adolescents are also subject to the decisions of their parents. For example, if parents move house the children have to move too, even if they have strong reasons for opposing the move. If there is a choice of school, parents probably make it.

The following extracts illustrate opposing attitudes to adolescent choice.

> . . . the right of freedom of choice about his school, college, curriculum and career . . . If the child finds himself unhappy at school, he should be able to expect his family's support in changing the conditions there, or moving to another.   (NCCL, ND, no. 4, p. 4)
>
> A child, by virtue of being a child, should not expect to be consulted about *any* decisions regarding his day-to-day life − it is frequently this misguided assumption that a child is capable of the responses of adulthood that has brought about his placement [in a CHE] in the first place.   (Howarth and Summers 1978)
>
> Boys at the Wildernesse School who imitate the 'skinhead' fashion by having their hair cut very short are being fined 5/- by the headmaster . . . [who] said that it was not the hairstyle which he disapproved of, but what the style signified; and that anti-social types are always portrayed as having either very long hair or very short hair. (*Sevenoaks News* 1970, in NCCL, ND, no. 1, p. 6)

Physical change

Being adolescent entails physical change and any such change may have associated problems, if only those of becoming accustomed to a new state. Voice change, growth of pubic and facial hair, development of hips, waist and breasts or testicles and penis, increased height, menarche and beginning of sexual potency and fertility; these add up to a lot of changing in a short time.

Since adolescents are minors until 18 there is no rite of passage to acknowledge the physical achievement of man- and womanhood at much earlier ages. The menarche may be greeted by the presentation of the first packet of sanitary towels and, in some households still, exhortations to keep anything to do with periods secret from the men of the family. Even in freer homes, rejoicing at the birth of the new woman is unlikely. To many women the period is known as 'the curse' and the menarche is perhaps for many the beginning only of 30 or 40 years' nuisance and discomfort. Many problems may accompany periods − pain, tension, sore breasts, depression, sluggishness, irregularity, the fear that blood has seeped through sanitary towel, pants and dress, the panic to get to the WC in time. Particularly if the girl lives in a family where shame is attached to sexuality and the period is regarded as dirty, the whole monthly experience may be physical and emotional torture. For boys, the nearest equivalent experience is nocturnal emission (wet dreams) which may cause anxiety and embarrassment.

Masturbation is not an involuntary change but is part of learning about the changing body and new sensations. This perfectly normal behaviour in boys and girls may stimulate not only orgasm but shame.

Puberty is marked by hair growth in various new places. To be glamorous or even decorous, girls shave off underarm and leg hair, and indeed, any hair which strays from the leg holes of a bathing costume. Female facial hair is regarded as ugly and even shameful. Boys can keep shaggy arms and chests which are, like facial hair, sources of pride and signs of manhood. But though school boys may keep their hairy arms and chests they may not have beards.

Accommodation

Most adolescents live in the homes of their parents and can expect to return there long after they eventually choose homes of their own. Not infrequently the bedroom of the former adolescent is still known as 'Bob's room' and is available for Bob long after he has left home. A 40-year-old friend referred to her mother's house as home, although my friend had left home over 20 years ago and her mother has lived in her present house for only two years.

In contrast many of the adolescents known to social workers are homeless (or at least rootless in the sense that their parental doors are forever closed to them) or living for a temporary period away from their parents. Peter has had no permanent home since leaving his parents, as he has moved between children's home, friends' flats and hostels. Dorna's residence in a foster home may be short lived as she moves towards independence in a bed-sitter, unable to fit in with family life after 16 years in numerous institutions.

The adolescent in care has lost, for a time at least, his family and has been through some bad experience; in custodial care he has committed some offence and has a difficult relationship with authority and society to sort out; in hospital he is or has been in pain and fear or is physically or mentally not deemed fit to live outside a medically focused establishment.

Other problems are connected with the basic need to find a bed for *tonight*. Eileen Eisenklam writes about Girls Alone in London Service (GALS), part of whose provision was 'a small and homely hostel [with] seven beds, where those girls who were destitute could be taken in immediately and offered supportive care aimed at getting them on to their feet' (Eisenklam 1978). She considers that 'a period of three months in such accommodation would give girls time for mature reflection of their actions and time to seek a job of their choice, rather than having to accept, because of financial needs, the first job that is offered'. Adolescents may find themselves in strange cities, homeless and penniless but they may also be homeless in their native city or extremely unhappy in their family home and longing for a new address.

John Hudson (1978) draws attention to

> school leavers who run into personal or social problems [and] find themselves in a limbo where none of the social services in their widest sense are willing or able to help out . . . though local authority housing departments will not accept school leavers as tenants, some are prepared to enter into arrangements with social services departments to accommodate some under-18s. But both housing and social services departments tend to refuse help to those who have left home of their own accord. [There is] for the young person who no longer has the security of a family . . . is subjected to violence at home . . . cannot find work near home and wants to move . . . has been in a CHE or a detention centre and has no home to return to . . . no great rush to help out.

At least when the adolescent is in care the social services department has a statutory duty to provide accommodation. But that accommodation may be far from satisfactory. A friend wrote to me of a point 'which is causing a lot of concern in our area . . . the lack of suitable residential facilities for adolescents . . . This is especially acute for girls who are over 13 where the only assessment centre (for girls in that age group) presents as something left over from the dark ages with peeling, graffiti-covered walls, locked doors, cells etc; and where girls coming for assessment for the first time may well be mixed with other very disturbed youngsters returning for their eighth or ninth session!'

In Chapter 4 I write about the headaches that shortage of suitable accommodation causes for social workers but the bodies-to-be-moved have problems too, not the least being that they must often feel just like that – bodies-to-be-moved. By the time a young person leaves care at 18 he may have been through nursery, foster home, assessment centre, one or two children's homes, perhaps another foster home (possibly at 16 when he leaves school – and why combine leaving school and home base?), perhaps a CHE, perhaps a hostel. In 1978 I wrote:

> Even if the move into new accommodation in mid-adolescence is

planned and well handled by all concerned, the adolescent may still experience this as another rejection. If the move involves any problems he is bound to feel anxious, confused and probably hostile and negative. For example, it must be dreadful to be advertised for, to know that you are due for a move but it is proving very difficult to find anyone to take you. Surely someone must want him, the adolescent thinks, and if not, surely that just confirms all he has felt about himself since his first rejection by his parents.

Then the adolescent is supposed to share the social worker's pleasure at somewhere being found, to co-operate in being introduced, at leaving what was at least some kind of safety and, at best, his home; leaving at worst because he is not wanted and at best because his bed is needed for someone else.

If the new carers fail the tests, the adolescent is confirmed in the view that all this welcoming and show of affection really is on the surface; he really is *not* wanted. (Crompton 1978a)

Being in care and leaving care

In recent years there has been much work, notably by the National Children's Bureau (NCB) (Page and Clark 1977) and Church of England Children's Society (Nelson and Seddon 1979), to learn from young people in care about their feelings and experiences. As I write work is in progress for an NCB study of young people leaving care.

Christian Wolmar (1980) quotes a hostel worker: 'suitable housing is probably the most vital requirement of a successful transition from care' and adds that 'It is even more important the young person is mentally equipped to deal with adulthood. It is the failure of local authorities to prepare adequately for this transition that is both their most important and easily remediable error.' He quotes Marcia: ' "In the home you never did a thing for yourself. It was a real treat if you were allowed to do a bit of hoovering or to peel the potatoes. We weren't briefed how to cope. We didn't expect these problems and when I came up against them I was really frightened." ' Dorna, a girl of great independence and initiative, hopes to live in a flat for the last few months of her life in care, not because she wants financial help from the local authority but because she needs to experience full independence while she is still in care and before she marries.

Children and adolescents in care are dependent on and subject to both the local authority (through its statutory responsibilities) and whoever has day-to-day care, whether residential staff or foster parents. On leaving care they are suddenly no-one's responsibility. Christian Wolmar notes that the help, including financial assistance, available under the provisions of the Children Act 1948, Section 20 (see now Child Care Act 1980, Section 27):

> . . . is a discretionary provision so the extent of its use varies widely among authorities.
>
> Birmingham, for example, with over 200 young people leaving care at the maximum age each year, only used section 20 money to help 18 people in 1978. Even then it was for educational purposes, for teenagers who had obviously coped well, and not to help with accommodation or other basic needs.   (Wolmar 1980)

Unemployment

'Young people', writes Philip Hope (National Council for Voluntary Organisations) 'want jobs, income, status and choice' (Hope 1981). 'What do you do?' is one of the first questions asked between newly-introduced people and status in this society does depend very greatly on employment. With neither status nor money, unemployed adolescents may perceive very little opportunity for choice.

If physically fit, averagely intelligent adolescents find job-finding difficult, the problem is far worse for those with some kind of disability. Diana Reynolds (1980) suggests that their problems may be increased by 'their often too sheltered upbringing (though many of them are in care or come from single-parent families)', unrealistic hopes – 'One young woman who recently completed a course of training at a special college for the disabled, found that "there were quite a few examples of people being put on training for work they would never be capable of doing" ' – and difficulties in feeling confident and presenting themselves at their best. 'It is up to teachers, social workers and parents to start preparing them now to get past their handicap and communicate.'

Despite race relations legislation, non-white school leavers too may expect extra difficulties in finding jobs.

Finding and starting work is often difficult for adolescents known to social workers even when jobs are abundant, for problems of family relationships, delinquency, health and so on may well be impediments. Young people already suffering from some kind of stigma are especially vulnerable. Here is Sheila, a 16-year old with a stormy history in care (I refer to Sheila further in Chapters 3, 4 and 5):

> Sheila's interview at the careers office was to be an extremely demoralising incident. Being a bright, intelligent girl, she had hopes of becoming a nurse or an office worker. Her interviewer cut the ground from under her feet when she looked at her hands and arms and said, 'With those tattoos, it's factory work or nothing.' Sheila swore at her, walked out of the office and gave up any determination to find work. (Parry 1980)

Neither would Dorna, also stigmatised by tattoos, dream of seeking employment without long-sleeved protection.

Offending

Many of the adolescents known to social workers will have been in some trouble with the police or at least have broken the law. Much social work time is devoted to seeking to prevent adolescents from committing further offences. Theories about the causes of delinquent behaviour abound, ranging from genetics to economics, subculture to separation. Children and young people who commit offences are seen variously as sick, deprived, vicious or desperate. Delinquent behaviour may constitute nothing more serious than stealing milk from doorsteps or cigarettes from supermarkets, or it may lead to 'the end of the jagged line of intervention' where the offenders have to be 'placed in a specialised, restrictive facility because they have pushed people responsible for them to the end of their tether' (Hoghughi 1978, p. 15). Either way, the offence may lead to a judgement that the offender needs welfare supervision or care or a punitive experience such as a fine or custodial sentence.

A major problem for adolescents who appear before juvenile courts is the attitude of the law to their offences. Perhaps most important is the age at which a person is deemed to be capable of wilfully committing an action known to be wrong. Despite the directive of the Children and Young Persons Act 1969 (HMSO) that the minimal age of criminal responsibility should be 12, in December 1981 it is still ten.

Many writers consider that the treatment afforded by juvenile courts to adolescents charged with the commission of offences is inconsistent and inequitable. This is partly because of the confusion which may arise from the dilemma of 'whether or not the court sees itself as a forum for justice or welfare' (Morris *et al*. 1980, p. 77). 'The requirements of justice can inhibit the imposition of treatment techniques and children tend to have few legal rights in courts with a welfare orientation' (p. 96).

Howard Parker and his colleagues (1981) consider that the juvenile court usually regards adolescents (12 to 17) and 'certainly once they are 14 . . . as culpable and largely responsible for their own actions . . . Yet to date there has been no systematic examination of the perceptions of such juveniles – the acid test about "care and control" has been avoided' (p. 1). (This study examines many aspects of juvenile justice including social and probation work.)

In a book sub-titled *The Unjust Treatment of Children in Courts and Institutions* Laurie Taylor and colleagues (1980) ask:

1. Is any coercive intervention which is proposed genuinely in the 'best interests of the child'?

2. To what extent is such intervention based not upon the personal characteristics of the child and parent but upon socio-economic circumstances beyond their control?

3. What opportunities exist for the child and his/her parent or representatives to question the decision which is allegedly made in his/her 'best interests'?

4. To what extent are those who propose intervention required to justify their claims by balancing the child's present situation against the likely results of institutionalisation?

5. In the event of children being removed from home and community to institution, what provisions exist for the maintenance of the basic rights they would enjoy outside that institution?   (pp. 10–11)

Glue and booze

Great concern is currently felt about the adolescents (and children) who are addicted to sniffing glue and other solvents. While this is not an offence in itself it can lead to delinquent acts and truancy. It is also a grave health risk. Dennis O'Connor, who runs a voluntary Saturday morning clinic for glue-sniffers, found that those who came to him had grave problems, usually within their homes, and Eva Merrill (1978) writes that

> Recent studies into case-histories of a number of glue-sniffing young-sters . . . indicated that in almost every case of persistent sniffing there had been marital problems between the parents and/or long-standing difficulties in family relationships.
> Simon's parents had fought and bickered all through his early child-hood, finally separating when he was nine years old. At adolescence he found his loyalties were still torn between his easy-going, unconventional and perhaps irresponsible mother, for whom he had a deep affection, and his rather staid and somewhat dull and pedantic father, who never-theless represented security . . . For him the strain of shuttling between two such different personalities left him drained and miserable. Glue-sniffing effectively blocked these problems out.

Dorna (Wilson) wrote an article in 1981 which

> is not a dig at glue-sniffers, it is merely to let them know just what it does to them. I also hope it will help their parents and mates to understand just how much attention they need while on glue . . . it's their way of saying HELP! . . .
> There is nothing clever about sniffing glue. It just goes to show your mind is sick and you have no will-power of your own. Instead of running

away from your problems face them and sort them out. Your life is what *YOU* make it – not the hallucinations. They're only a decoy, because afterwards the problems are still there, aren't they?

Glue-sniffing may be a means to escape. It is probably also a way of getting status with peers. Jimmy Boyle writes of his life in the Gorbals, where at 14 he and his friends would steal in order to buy alcohol:

> Boozing became a big thing for us and when we got drunk we would do crazy things like smashing shop windows and fighting . . . Our stealing was now for booze money and there would be time when we would be going into school with a hangover and bleary eyes. Kids at fifteen would try to bluff their way into the pubs and be turned back and we would be sitting there a year younger, getting away with it. These were the things that I and my pals valued most . . . all of us were going around becoming near-alcoholics at the age of fourteen. The pitiful side of it all is that never at any time did I get the least pleasure from drinking. I really didn't like the stuff, but drinking was the done thing so I did it. (Boyle 1977, pp. 59–60)

Sex

A prized freedom in Great Britain is that of hetero- and homosexual intercourse between consenting adults, irrespective of marriage (adherence to some particular moral code may impose restraint but there is no legal impediment). Many Westerners regard with horror the fierce penalties exacted for sexual misdemeanour in, for example, Iran. But our belief in freedom is not extended to heterosexual girls under 16, boys under 14 and homosexuals under 21 (although legal adulthood begins at 18).

The NCCL declares

> The right of young people to have sexual relations as soon as they wish . . . most important . . . and of course carries with it the right to constructive information, advice and equipment . . . [and] a higher degree of privacy than is generally available to young people today. (NCCL, ND, no. 4, p. 6)

Leonard Davis (1980) advocates reduction of the age of consent to 15 or even 14 because 'a comparatively high level of sexual activity among the under-16s is a fact and the present law does relatively little to lessen it' and he does not expect adolescents unprotected by the law to engage in sexual intercourse before they feel ready. Another reason he gives is that 'the uncertainty relating to contraceptive advice' and supply for under-16s puts large numbers of adults and young people into ambiguous positions. He quotes the DHSS *Memorandum of Guidance*:

It is for the doctor to decide whether to provide contraceptive advice and treatment, and . . . if he does so for a girl under 16, he is not acting unlawfully, provided he acts in good faith in protecting the girl against the potentially harmful effects of intercourse. (Department of Health and Social Security 1974)

'Other professional workers' who help to procure contraception for an under 16-year old are also cleared of 'acting unlawfully'. In other words, it is illegal for the girl to have sexual intercourse but she may legally be aided to prevent conception. Leonard Davis considers that 'the operation of law as it stands, both as a deterrent and an instrument of punishment, has almost ceased to exist'. A disregarded law exposes the law as a whole to disrepute. (See also pp. 48–9.)

Pregnancy: Angela Willans regards pregnancy as a 'fringe benefit' of sex: 'What seems to be an utterly irresponsible act may, in fact, be a way of gaining adult responsibilities that are witheld for too long.' Or it may be a way of escaping from school boredom and college pressures (Willans 1977, p. 113).

Whatever the reason for conception, pregnant schoolgirls may have a rough ride from parents and schools. Alan Hazell, a Cambridgeshire Education Welfare Officer, reported that he 'found no evidence that pupils are adversely affected by the presence of pregnant girls in schools' but that girls were often told to leave on an arbitrary date on grounds of 'convenience and discipline' (British Association of Social Workers [BASW] 1980).

Not only adults adopt a punitive approach to adolescent mothers – and indeed, fathers. Writing about work with a group of adolescents in care, Penny Gutridge (1970) records:

Before long the first suspected pregnancy set the household agog, and pretty soon there was division between those wholly in sympathy with the supposed mother to be, and those who roundly condemned her as an ignorant mug for 'getting caught'.

Incest: when interviewing social workers in preparation for this book, I was surprised at the number of times incest was mentioned. This is still, I think, almost *un*mentionable in Great Britain and the horror derived from the taboo may inhibit adolescents from seeking confidants. While actual or made-up sexual experience may be a source of status, incest, whether with parent or sibling, is not something to boast about. This 'widespread but hidden problem' is well introduced in an article by Elinor Harbridge (1981). Dennis O'Connor told me that a significant number of the young people referred (by self or a third person) to his clinic for solvent abuse had experienced incest and been unable to obtain any help, either because they could not speak of it or because their own families took the side of the guilty relative (in these cases always male). One girl whose stepfather abused her was herself rejected by her family because her evidence led to the man's imprisonment.

Venereal disease: VD is, like pregnancy, the source of much adult fear about adolescent sexual activity. Modern treatments have enormously reduced the danger associated with the illnesses classed as VD but they are still extremely unpleasant. As with incest, shame, ignorance and fear may inhibit the adolescent from obtaining help.

Race: despite parliamentary acts against racial discrimination, black, yellow and brown skinned people are still regarded and treated by many with pink skins as inferior, even scarcely human. Coloured adolescents may well have been born in Great Britain and speak with the accents of Birmingham and Brixton rather than Barbados and Bombay. Others may be recent immigrants, faced with upheaval from settled childhoods often to join scarcely known parents in a strange country. Eileen Eisenklam (1978) found that the girls from the West Indies who came to GALS 'had to adapt to living in two cultures and submit to Victorian standards laid down by their parents. Breakdown in family life was evident.'

Feeling adolescent
Between 12 and 19 every individual experiences dramatic change. And while each person's feelings about that change, from childhood to adulthood, must be unique, it is possible and useful to consider some of the areas of feeling which may be common to many if not all adolescents.

Am I normal?
In Chapter 1 Jo spoke of her creeping and not-understood unhappiness at 15 as she realised that while she no longer wanted to play with children, she was not yet fully accepted in adult conversations. At 17 she was confident enough to plan a future of training including a year between school and college, had made friends and a strong commitment to peace work, and regularly attended a religious meeting. Some of her difficulties came from isolation, for although she could talk freely with her parents she had no reinforcement of her normality outside the home. And since becoming adult involves increasing interaction with the world of adults other than parents this is very important.

Like Jo, I was reared in a stable middle-class home and I too suffered from a sense of oddness. I longed to be ordinary, imagining that all my friends were 'normal'. Like Jo, I should have been helped by having my normality (including that of feeling odd) reinforced. It is easy, and dangerous, to think that only adolescents in abnormal circumstances are victim to such doubts – young people like Sheila, 'a damaged young woman who for many years to come will suffer the consequences of the quality of her care in childhood and adolescence' and whose 'acknowledged ambition' is 'to be normal' (Parry 1980). Bruce Hugman (1977), working as a detached probation officer in the back streets of Sheffield, found that 'freed from some of life's emotional and practical snares what people wanted was often very conventional' (p. 46). Being 'conventional' may involve having an idea not only of who you are as an individual but also as a member of a family. Clare Wendelken (1981), writing on a search for the siblings of some adolescents in care says 'as part of the searching for who one is, it is common for teenagers to want to know more about their families and yet feel hesitant about asking, confused by the problems of integrating the bad past with their current selves'. (People of any age may long to find lost siblings, parents and other relatives; a friend of over 30 was told that her older half-sister had been adopted before her own birth – she will now never cease to wonder where is her sister, what is she like, should she try to find her?) Not only the adolescents known to Paul McKeever suffer 'a sense of "apartness", of being different from "normal" people. Most kids at some point expressed concern about being "a bit mad"' (1979, p. 15).

Loneliness and love
Few things are more conducive to loneliness than feeling abnormal because this is probably associated with feeling unloveable and unable to trust other people. Much behaviour at any time of life is directed to making friendships or collecting acquaintances. People who don't easily make friends may 'buy' friendship – drinks in the pub, presents, invitations, sex. Or they may join an interest group or class, or advertise in a magazine. But nothing can substitute for the sense of being liked or loved solely for your own sake. Sheila, desperate for affection, said to her social worker 'I know you care, but you are paid to care' (Parry 1980). It is humiliating to feel that the only person to care for you is simply doing her job. The highest praise Peter could give was to his former headmistress who 'cared not just because she was meant to – she *did* care'.

Yet many adolescents may experience at the least disapproval when they find affection and love. 'Denise', for example, was taken into care at 13 because she had intercourse with her boyfriend 'Don'. Eventually she absconded with him 'and played the house-wife quite efficiently, passing for an 18-year old with the help of the nice clothes he bought her and some make-up'. But at 15 and a half she was returned to care and Don imprisoned for unlawful sexual intercourse. 'By the time he came out she was 16. Her social workers tried to obtain the Director of Social Services' permission to allow her to marry.' As this was refused, she absconded and lived with Don until they could legally marry. As Emily Engel says in her letter to me, 'A happy ending for them, but a poor comment on society?', for the refusal of authority to recognise the seriousness and importance of Denise's relationship with Don cost her three years' schooling and a great deal of upheaval.

Denise was in many ways lucky, for not everyone can either express or receive affection. It is just as important to have an outlet, to be able to give, as it is to be able to receive, 'especially when the givers are those who have felt for so long that they have nothing to give to anyone' (Hugman 1977, pp. 48–9). William Glasser (1975) identifies 'two basic psychological needs: *the need to love and be loved and the need to feel that we are worthwhile to ourselves and to others*' (pp. 9–10). Would Peter, as I write, be awaiting trial on several charges if anyone had enabled him to feel worthwhile enough to give and receive love?

Worthlessness, depression, guilt and stigma
How difficult it is for even mature adults 'to feel that we are worthwhile to ourselves and others' (Glasser 1975, p. 10)! Many of us try to prove our worth through income, possessions or good works. Adolescents in trouble are particularly vulnerable to be-lieving in worthlessness for they have little opportunity to prove themselves otherwise, whether through activity or simply 'being'. Some may overwork at examinations, proving at least academic skill, others may strive to excel at games. But for many young people excellence cannot be achieved in any field.

These extracts are from an excellent book on Intermediate Treatment (IT) in Wandsworth (Leggett 1979):

> most of the children referred to us . . . could see little meaning in their lives. They seemed resigned to 'failure', had low self-esteem, and suffered because there were very few positive inputs from either home, school, work or leisure. (p. 6)

Many of the kids were contemptuous of schools and adults generally, but it was contempt fired by a sense of bitterness and loss – the kids yearned to belong, and, for all kids, the central 'belonging' place . . . is school. They felt cheated. And with reason: it was made clear to us that . . . no matter in what ways particular kids changed, they would be expelled on sight from their schools if they ever tried to go back.   (McKeever 1979, p. 15)

In other words these adolescents have no hope of gaining the approval of authority however much they behave 'properly'. Echoes of the girl brought up in care who asked Tom Hart (1979) to 'Give us hope for the future . . . by the time we get to you we feel so bad that all we really want to do is to lie down and die.'

Despair, depression, futility: painful emotions common to all humanity and as real in adolescence as at any other time. One boy experienced a struggle

whether to abandon home altogether or to bow to a dominant step-father. He decided to do neither. He faced them both, and himself, and by doing so grew more quickly than he bargained for. From being a recalcitrant child he became a pained and pensive adolescent with not enough sense of security. At least he has broken the theme of competitiveness with his stepfather, *but his anger has turned in on itself* and he describes his depression as less to do with people around him than with his own destiny.   (Hall 1979, p. 28; my italics)

This boy was living in a Scottish List D school (CHE) and from my conversations with Dorna I know that such depression is common. Children and young people in care or otherwise away from their natural families are particularly vulnerable to a sense of worthlessness and depression. For one thing they may have been rejected not only by their own families but also by professional carers. Penny Gutridge (1970) describes

a seemingly interminable procession of unhappy frightened girls, in-variably aggressive and defiant until out of sight of the last failure, then would come the tears and that awful bitterness: and so on to the next stop on the merry-go-round of brinkmanship. With each failure becoming more self-absorbed, self-pitying and self-destructive. Forever pursuing the elusive 'good time' they feel to be their birthright and mistakenly believing everyone else but themselves to be enjoying.

It is not far from this to the sense of *guilt* expressed by Dorna based on the belief inculcated by years of 'getting it wrong' and by the initial rejection by natural parents (for whatever reason). *Feeling* guilty is different from *being* guilty. *Feeling* guilty is pervasive and destructive and has, to my mind, very little to do with the development of a sense of responsibility. The guilt experienced by Dorna and her colleagues eats away at the development of self-esteem and confidence. It whispers all the time 'You really are bad.'

Mark Rayman's struggle to find himself and someone really to care about him led him eventually to an assessment centre where he asked himself ' "I have done nothing wrong to be locked up. Is this where care orders lead?" It had all started when I was six years and was supposed to have been a way of helping me – now it had drastically changed.' He felt that he was being treated as a bad person but had, like Dorna, the strength to develop a sense of self-esteem. When at last the care order was discharged it 'was like having a heavy load lifted from me – it felt so good to be free of the stigma. It was like being born again with a new independent life ahead of me' (Rayman 1979). A sense of *stigma* is all too familiar to children and young people in care, marked by their place of residence as 'different' and possibly 'bad'. Dorna recalled her first day in a new school. 'We must all be especially nice to Dorna as she's in the children's home', said the teacher. Dorna found this intolerable and in double-quick time had behaved so badly that she was expelled. She says that the teacher's attitude made her feel guilty and stigmatised.

Stigma is familiar, too, to those suffering some disability, whether physical or mental, and to those literally marked by colour or language. And for some adolescents, stigma attaches simply to *being* adolescent.

Respect and responsibility

'You robbed me of the chance to be responsible for my actions.'
(Bazalgette 1978)

the main responsibility for a person's behaviour and attitude rests with the person himself. Therefore any changes in a kid are to his own credit. (McKeever 1979, p. 17)

They found it hard to accept that the children had a way of life that was important to them. (Wendelken 1981)

The first extract is an accusation by a boy at a conference of the Association for the Psychiatric Study of Adolescents. 'By making him "a client" related to a "social worker" he was prevented from exploring what it meant to be a responsible citizen' (Bazalgette 1978).

The work of Paul McKeever, based on the attitude expressed in the second quotation, is perhaps unusual in a society concerned with denying the rights and abilities of many sections of its population. The idea that 'any changes in a kid are to his own credit' must reek of heresy to some, for how many adults really believe that children have 'a way of life that [is] important to them'?

How much are adolescents in care or hospital really consulted about their wishes and plans? How much are adolescents involved in the running of their schools and places of work?

Our village recently set up a community association and a committee was formed at the end of a very lively public meeting attended by residents of all ages from about eight to 80. There were no elections; anyone interested could join the committee or become a helper simply by signing on. Two teenage girls were showing interest and were obviously delighted when I invited them to join; they asked if two friends might join, too. For me this was the greatest triumph of an exciting evening. But next day a teacher telephoned. She was furious that 'children' had been taken onto the committee for they would have 'no ideas'. She was certain of this since, she said, she herself had taught them! But even if this were true, how can the girls learn how to frame and use ideas if always excluded from 'adult' pursuits?

In Poland in 1981, I visited the headquarters of a society devoted to the care and welfare of children based on the self-management practices of Janusz Korczak. A children's village, where life and education will be conducted according to these ideas is planned at Łomianki, near Warsaw. I asked if young people were involved in the planning. No, I was told, for they would lack specialist knowledge, and although some may attend special camps where they are told what is going on, active participation is limited to help with choosing furnishings. Eventually the Łomianki campus is to include an area where the children may build their own huts, bird-tables and other *temporary* structures.

Control and authority

For those adolescents who are struggling to discover who they are inside, as well as to establish a place in the world, it is probably very difficult to feel really in command of the self. While no emotion can outdo the rage of an unfed baby, adolescents may be surprised by strong passions. These experiences may be very frightening, and learning not to fear aggression and hate but to control them very difficult. Sheila, helped by Mair Parry, made the effort:

> For the first time [she] had made a major decision for herself. She wanted to go to the unit and to work on her problems herself. I took Sheila to and from the unit several times and was able to watch her reactions closely. At the beginning she was very apprehensive and could not understand

how these new authority figures were trying to treat her. She had no trust in them and could not accept their open, honest treatment of her at face value.

Very gradually she came to see that no one was trying to deceive her or treat her like a child. In this atmosphere *she learned that if anyone was going to control her aggression, it was herself.*(Parry 1980; my italics)

Some adolescents, far from needing to control aggression, endeavour to control their real softness under a veneer of toughness:

He presents himself as a 'hard' man because he believes it to be an effective image; if the effect he desires is not created, then he is considerably disarmed . . . a newcomer had spent a couple of days flexing his muscles. A very pretty girl whom he was clearly eager to impress addressed the world generally in a very tired, bored voice: *'The trouble with all them tough guys is that they're all little babies inside.'* Collapse of image.   (McKeever 1979, p. 17)

And collapse of sense of control! The pretty girl was exercising control, consciously deflating the boy's self-image.

Everyone is subject to control by someone but adolescents and children are subject to more control by more people than most of us – more control *by* other people coupled with less *of* other people, and of their own circumstances and environment. Some people may accept external control and authority without question but for many, particularly those who come into conflict with authority, it is difficult, if not impossible, to submit. Boys at Kneesworth Hall, a CHE for gifted delinquents

resisted anything perceived as coercion and were suspicious of any influences which emanated from their parents and teachers . . . a great deal of their behaviour was not so much a direct confrontation with society as the dismissal of the demands of parents and teachers as being perceived as irrelevant to their needs and self-fulfilment . . . Some of them found the models to which they were expected to conform profoundly dissatisfying and thoroughly constricting. (Brooks 1980, p. 3)

Rob Grunsell, running an IT centre in North London, found that

Anger against authority abounds in our area – against parents, against the police, the courts, the teachers. But so often it's an anger so confused that it can only bring self-destruction. Anger against repressive parents . . . anger at the absence of parental authority becomes so tangled up with genuine social anger about bad housing, police injustice, arbitrary authority in all its forms that it is impossible for the kids to govern their relationship to authority in their own best interests.(Grunsell, ND, p. 26)

The 'kids need and demand authority'; they experienced anger against both 'repressive parents' and 'absence of parental authority'. The development of balanced inner controls requires balanced and reasonable external controls, providing safe limits and the suggestion that someone cares enough to set them.

> To threaten a confused fifteen year old with a thick ear . . . can be the most helpful thing I can do. He can step back from testing the limits to explore his own confusions, safe in the knowledge that there is someone physically stronger to protect him from the most extreme oscillations of his behaviour.

(Although I agree with Rob Grunsell's comments on limit-setting, I am not myself in favour of thick-ear-threatening or, as must presumably sometimes follow, thick-ear-giving.)

Lesley, aged 15, remained on the run for many weeks until she 'arranged' to be found by walking past a central city police station in the middle of the night. She was placed in a remand home and

> . . . was relaxed and relieved. At last the door had closed on her and she was prevented from the terrifying quest for her own limits. Authority was saying 'no' and meaning it – and feeding and clothing and educating her. She had a chance to rest, to gather herself . . . in a way to be born again . . .
>
> Lesley was placed in [a CHE]. She was held and cared for by the Salvation Army officers who ran it, even when, after the expiry of the order, she left their voluntary after-care hostel and produced a baby. By the age of 18, Lesley had begun to achieve what looked like very efficient personal control and a sense of her own identity. Her previous adventures had ensured that she kept strong external controls while she still needed them. (Crompton 1978b)

Fun

In this chapter I have suggested some of the experiences which may provide problems for adolescents. But I am constantly conscious of Margaret Robinson's criticism of the book on adolescents which failed to show 'the vitality of the young people' (1981) and of Eddie Leggett's note that adolescents need 'to have a bit of fun' (1979, p. 9). Life may be rather grim and earnest, especially for young people in care or hospital, in trouble with the police or amidst severe family problems. Their mothers told the teenage girls that they must not giggle at the community association committee meetings – but the odd giggle might improve our rather intense proceedings.

Here are some very vital young people on an outing with David Harris, a residential social worker:

> 'We'll just walk naturally to the station' I said naively . . . I should have known better.
> That walk to the station was a disaster. The boys really entered into the

spirit of the occasion. Instead of 'walking naturally' they formed an orderly line behind me, stopped when I stopped, coughed when I coughed, and generally goose-stepped through the shopping centre.

Once on the train

'We're the hostel lads' announced Johnny to a full carriage of passengers. 'We're all triple murderers' shouted Mike, following the lead. 'Watch your handbag, missus', was Keith's contribution, 'We're all with him.' (1979)

Expectations
Independence
Physical Change
Accommodation
Care
Unempt
Drugs
Sex
Feelings:
    love
    loneliness
    stigma
    guilt
    depression

Respect & Responsibility
Control o
Authority

} CAN CAUSE ADO's Problems!

4 Social Workers: Feelings and Experiences

> It is quite untenable for a field social worker, who appears infrequently and then usually only when there is trouble, to have a major responsibility for making the arrangements for the life of a child growing up in care.
>
> (James 1979, pp. 64–5)

This discouraging comment leads straight to the core of some of the problems of field social workers working with adolescents. Are they really competent even to try? Gwen James was writing about work with children in care, but her point has relevance for every area of social work. In this chapter, I suggest some of the feelings and experiences which may inhibit social workers from even trying to work with adolescent clients.

Discouragement

The strongest discouragement to offering successful help to another person is, I suspect, simple dislike. It may be easy enough to hand over money or make straightforward practical arrangements but setting out to form a helping relationship surely requires some measure of liking. And it is quite possible to dislike individuals not only as themselves but also as representatives of groups, for example prostitutes, black men, old people, adolescents. There is no shame in *feeling* dislike but there is danger in *not recognising* it: the result may be distortions in contact such as overcompensation or rejection.

Social workers may not like working with adolescents even if they do not dislike adolescents themselves, because of the discouragement of feeling *inadequate* and *impotent*; so often so little can be done. 'Most people', says Bruce Hugman, 'feel they have little freedom to change the accepted order of things' (1977, p. 10), and the problems of adolescents may seem particularly intransigent. It is very easy to be discouraged from even starting because the task seems too great and the social worker sets herself too much to achieve. Josephine Klein writes:

> There is something about defining oneself as a helpful person, especially if one is paid a salary for it, which easily throws people off balance. Internal and external pressures combine to make one feel at the same time *arrogant* and *inadequate*. For instance, one might feel one ought to present a very knowledgeable front while in a *constant panic that one will not know enough to understand or help*. (1973, p. 15; my italics)

Such a 'constant panic' may erect an impenetrable barrier between social worker and adolescent.

It may also contribute to the development of that killer, *guilt*. The feelings of this hypothetical teacher are equally recognisable in social work:

> . . . drained by the adolescent's excessive demands and resentful of [his] unreasonableness and ingratitude, his whole self-esteem as a helping, caring adult and teacher is undermined. It appears that there is no way he can succeed in getting through to the adolescent student. He is left with feelings of *inadequacy – feeling as useless and unwanted as the adolescent himself may feel – and guilty*. These are painful feelings and in defence the teacher understandably may turn away; either ignoring or resorting to blaming or punishing the adolescent . . .
>
> There is often a sense of *shame* in admitting the kinds of feelings we have indicated as if there pervades within the culture of many schools a persistent ideal that the teacher should at all times achieve the virtues of control, fairness and benign intention. This ideal clearly does not fit with the reality, that all *teachers are people with personal vulnerabilities* . . .
>
> (Wilson and Bottomley 1980, p. 19 and p. 23; my italics)

Inadequacy, guilt, shame – no wonder that in social work 'we are often tempted to draw boundaries around ourselves in a rigid and protective way, a way that smells of fear' (Brandon 1979, p. 33). The social worker may delude herself that she is working against tremendous odds for the best interests of a very difficult client while failing to recognise that much of the difficulty in the encounter stems from her own defences against him. William (Bill) Jordan writes of 'defensive rules of thumb' which can 'help the worker to defend himself against the often negative (though occasionally strongly positive) feelings which . . . clients arouse within him'; he suggests that 'it is the worker's ego rather than the client's that may be under threat' (Jordan 1970, pp. 47–8).

In the remainder of this chapter, I suggest some of the feelings and experiences which may cause the worker to feel under threat.

Material help

On the preceding page I said 'It may be easy enough to hand over money or make straightforward practical arrangements', but now I must add that it may often be extremely difficult to do either because of the shortage of material resources available to social workers. If anything is discouraging it is having to say 'No, sorry.' The difficulty of obtaining resources may discourage social workers from even trying, and those who do keep seeking jobs and accommodation and so on may feel that they bear a crippling burden. Any of Penny Gutridge's 'depressed and frustrated CCO's' [child care officers] who 'coped almost daily with outraged land-ladies, those "last straws" and sudden grim departures that followed' (1970) might have written with me 'I do not believe I am the only person ever to have breathed a sigh of relief because a teenage member of my caseload had an official bed – any bed – even though the whole search might have to start again next week' (Crompton 1978a).

Under constant pressures to provide a solution it is often tempting to make do with whatever comes to hand, to disregard William Glasser's exhortation 'always be strong, never expedient' (1975, p. 27). One way of being expedient may be to ignore, deliberately or otherwise, the real and pressing importance of the practical need and to concentrate on the client's emotions. I am shocked to realise that it never occurred to me how depressing and debilitating are the effects of too little food and rest. *I* became tired and depressed if I lacked regular and large meals and plenty of sleep, but I did not apply the same standards to the worn-out mothers I saw every day. I 'bought' the image of them as inadequate, poor managers, depressed, without considering what a difference would be made by a few square meals, cooked and served by someone else and eaten sitting down and in quiet, plus unbroken sleep on a comfortable bed.

Practical problems may be undervalued for more positive reasons. Linda Hill writing on counselling suggests that:

> Young people frequently use a request for information as a way of asking for help that may conceal more complex underlying needs – however, if presented with a request for a leaflet, I will give the young person a leaflet, whilst being sensitive and open to other unspoken needs. *I believe that treating every enquiry as a request for counselling is patronising to young people* ...   (Hill 1980, p. 10; my italics)

Josephine Klein offers another warning:

> The workers most profoundly affected by the ideology of autonomy and creativity tend to underestimate the damage done by bad housing, lack of play-encouragement, authoritarian schooling and employment, etc. Or maybe they tend to over-estimate the ease with which such damage can be undone. In their respect for others they thus may miss opportunities.   (Klein 1973, p. 10)

Behaving responsibly

In 1978 Roy Howarth and James Summers, workers in a senior boarding school for maladjusted boys, criticised an interpretation of Section 12 of the 1975 Children Act (on consulting children about their views) as being

> ... an open-ended route by which the social worker, uncertain of his social or moral precepts, may escape the responsibility of making admittedly difficult, but necessary, adult decisions in the interests of his client. It further enables him to have a clear conscience in doing so ... the directionless character of child care at present ... precipitates, even forces, such abrogation of professional responsibility.

The writers call for a 'firm base of clearly understood values and standards' and supply a prescription 'to condemn theft, anti-social behaviour and a contempt for the welfare of other individuals around him'. I doubt if condemning anything, except a dangerous building, brings positive results and I do not agree that the involvement of children in decision-making implies that social workers are necessarily or even probably abrogating their responsibilities. But the strongly-held views of the writers surely reflect those of many other workers.

It is difficult enough to work out and live by a code of 'clearly understood values and standards' in one's own life without representing such a code to people from different backgrounds and experiences. But it is a serious matter if, as psychologist Ron Pidduck (1981) suggests,

> ... social workers in the community do not very often discuss with their clients ... why teenage boys [and girls] get into trouble and also possible ways ... in which they can try to keep out of trouble. It is as if everyone assumes either that there is just no solution to stealing so there is no point in talking about it, or ... that as long as we provide the best child care and education ... the delinquent aspects of our boys will automatically fade away.

He adds 'Let us not underestimate teenagers' capacity to think certain things out' and concludes:

> We degrade ourselves ... when we underestimate our capacity to act honestly and to express honest ideas and attitudes, and especially when we pretend that man does not have, or cannot have, certain definite moral values in relation to stealing and ... to so many other issues. . .
>
> (Pidduck 1981)

Social workers are constantly faced with 'immorality', and however 'open' and unconstrained by convention they may wish or consider themselves to be, there is no escape from the fact that their 'decisions are essentially moral ones' and that 'their moral judgement [has] a profound influence'. Elinor Harbridge (1981), quoted here, is writing about a case of incest involving a young adolescent girl and sees the essentially moral character of social workers' decisions as a constraint.

One problem may be knowing just what is one's own moral code or, as John Bazalgette (1978) says, 'I found myself agonising over how to behave responsibly' and 'How do I know when I am behaving with integrity?' He suggests that 'we lose our *integrity* . . . when we lose our capacity to identify with our role in the whole of society – our role as a citizen – but identify with one part to the exclusion of other parts'. He tells of social workers who became involved with a boy who had killed another in a fight. At the police station 'They were loud with their advice to the boy and his mother, they were openly hostile to the "pigs" and the whole business was a furore for some hours.' Much later it was realised that 'though many social workers had been intensely active with the defendent and his family, no-one from Social Services had made contact with the family of the dead boy, though they also lived in the team's area.' John Bazalgette considers that the social workers had 'lost their integrity . . . a conception of themselves as *responsible citizens* and members of a whole which contains persecutors, victims and rescuers; they had identified with one part against another part'. It would have been an equal betrayal of integrity to have condemned the violent boy, failing to pay attention to his needs. But the failure even to think about the dead boy's family is shocking.

John Bazalgette's illustration sets out a stark story of lost integrity and unsatisfactory moral code. Most social workers will not be faced with so dramatic a test but it is a useful parable which draws together some of the other points in this section.

The outside world

Social workers must often feel that the 'outside world' in the form of Acts of Parliament, courts, police, schools, press, the public and their bosses expect them to be not only omnipotent but also, like God, omniscient and omnipresent. (Their own consciences often expect this, too.) I felt that the police expected me to be a patrolling chastity belt, keeping the adolescent girls on my patch out of 'trouble' and being personally responsible if they got into it. Inquests on battered children may emphasise the inadequacy of social work supervision and decisions, but satisfactory work makes no headlines.

Since, I think, social workers are identified with their clients in the public mind – and their clients are by definition unlikely to be valued or respected members of society – the pressures and expectations from that society for impossibly high results to be achieved with impossibly low resources are all but unbearable.

Social workers are required to find accommodation and jobs, prevent truanting, improve self-images and family relationships, inhibit delinquency, drug-taking and glue-sniffing, stop unlawful sexual intercourse and under-age pregnancies, counsel about adoption and abortion, loneliness, unhappiness – all this in often poor working conditions with the further requirement to maintain good contact with anyone else interested in the client.

Relationships with other workers may prove a considerable problem. Dislike is again important, for co-operation is not easy if the co-operators cannot stand one another. It is at least necessary to understand what causes the dislike (e.g. opinions, manner, hair colour, resemblance to a former spouse or employer). One source of discord may be professional mistrust, probably based on ignorance. How many social workers assume that they know what teachers do? But how many have been teachers or spent any time since the age of 18 in a school? And how many teachers think they know about social workers, basing their knowledge on, perhaps, experience of one social worker and one case, or even media publicity? Rosemary Dinnage, who spent some time as a social worker within a boys' comprehensive school, summarises some of the problems of the teacher in making, or rather not making, a referral and then says that

> . . . working as a social worker, one often bemoans the late referral of children with difficulties when in a sense the problem is a *fait accompli* and attitudes have hardened so much that a miracle worker is needed, not a social worker. It is not surprising that there is hostility or at least distrust between the two professions.   (Dinnage 1978)

Hostility must certainly have been felt by Mair Parry when the careers advisor told Sheila 'With those tattoos, it's factory work or nothing.' And such an experience where the helping social worker expected her client to trust another helper who proved to be untrustworthy could have damaged the girl's trust in the social worker herself. What could Mair Parry have done to improve co-operation with the careers adviser?

Relationships between residential (nursing or care) and field staff are notorious minefields. Here as elsewhere ignorance of one another's jobs, with their pressures and skills, surely plays a large part, inhibiting the development of respect and fostering jealousies. Despite much improvement in recent years medical staff are still not unanimous in their acceptance and use of social workers. And I know that many residential staff still feel that they are regarded by field staff as 'thick', fit to cope with day to day caring but not to take more than a lip-service part in decision making. When staff cannot co-operate, respect one another and fulfil each her own task in her own best way, the client or patient is the loser and he may have very little to lose. Dennis Dobson writes that the consequence of

> . . . a split between those making decisions (primarily social workers) and those holding resources, e.g. IT workers, residential workers, group workers, youth workers and others . . . is a failure to use existing resources or effectively introduce clients to the most appropriate resource [because the] hard-pressed social worker . . . is not able to satisfactorily hold the 'key worker' and decision-making role with all his clients.   (Dobson 1979, p. 33)

The concept of the 'key worker' itself poses problems. For example, with a child or adolescent in care:

> Does this mean that the field worker . . . abdicates responsibility for the care of the child to residential staff? Or . . . that the residential social worker is asked to pursue his work with the child as an agent of the field social worker? Or . . . that the field social worker delegates responsibility to the residential worker?   (Howells, 1978)

I have devoted much precious space to this topic if only to reflect the amount of time social workers must spend on 'public relationships' on behalf of their clients, especially those whose voices receive little attention in the 'outside world'.

Who cares for the social worker?

At my interview for a post as child care officer in 1965 I asked if there would be any supervision. A lady councillor enthusiastically thought I wanted to supervise students. Her enthusiasm disappeared when I explained that the supervision was for *me* and I nearly did not get the job. She thought I could not be competent if I still needed help. I was 24 and still training – but I should ask the same question now. Linda Hill agrees: 'The counsellor should be very self-aware and constantly questioning; regular access to a good supervisor and consultant is essential' (1980, p. 11).

Although I hope and believe that support and supervision – and consultation – are far more available now than in the mid-1960s I do *not* think that many social workers receive anything like enough and Peter Mortimore (Director of Research and Statistics for the Inner London Education Authority) might be surprised from his view that the lack of staffroom help for teachers 'contrasts with that of other professional groups. In medicine, social work and educational psychology newly qualified practitioners are under close supervision and asking for help, in the form of a second opinion, is normal practice' (Mortimore 1980, p. 9).

Social workers need the care, help and encouragement which they are expected to give to clients. If adolescents need help to feel valued and valuable, achieving and useful, so do their social workers.

The social worker's own life

I have referred to the impact of each individual's own experience of both her adolescence and present life on her perception of and attitude towards adolescence. The feelings and attitudes of the social worker have much influence on her work and may bring problems.

Linda Hill writes 'In many of the counselling relationships I have had, experiences of my own adolescence have been revived' and although she has learned how to use this for the benefit of the clients she warns that 'There can be a danger of over-identifying, and being unhelpful to the client' (1980, p. 11). *Collusion* is a great danger in work with adolescents. Wilson and Bottomley suggest that 'If [the teacher's] own adolescence has been a time of unhappiness, confusion and desperate rebellion, he will be more inclined to empathise or perhaps over identify with these characteristics in his students' (1980, p. 22). They suggest other handicapping effects of personal attitudes towards adolescence not properly understood and dealt with:

> . . . the adult's envy of the more progressive, expansive aspects of adolescence can give rise to considerable ambivalence in the adult; either deriving enjoyment from his students' youthful vigour and experimentation or in subtle ways choosing to attack and begrudge their adolescence. (1980, p. 22)

It is particularly important to be aware of any unresolved problems from one's own adolescence, for example continuing over-dependence on or resentment of a parent. And one area of difficulty which may well arise in adolescence and persist into adulthood is that of *sex*. I suppose that few people avoid some problem regarding sex whether it be shame and distaste at the onset of puberty, difficulty in achieving orgasm, fantasies about 'perfect' sex and one's own apparent shortcomings, impotence or frigidity (permanent or temporary) or just occasional boredom. I do not think I ever discussed sex with staff or students under my supervision and yet some at least must have been experiencing some kind of sexual problem, as must many of their clients. Although I do not believe that *having* an experience is essential if a social worker is to offer understanding and help I do think that we should feel able at least to gain vicarious experience even if only through talking. How much, for example, *can* a young virgin *really* understand about excessive sexual demands from a possibly violent man? Or about how it feels to be pregnant for the sixth time and a Roman Catholic? Or about being pregnant for the first time and aged 14? I am a 40-year old childless woman with a gentle and loving husband and I know that *I* do not really understand. But now I can recognise that I do not and could if necessary acknowledge that to both supervisor and client and try to learn how my lack of knowledge and understanding affected my social working. And I can recall from my own practice how my childlessness and the problems of my first marriage affected my attitude towards, for example, adoption work. I was very reluctant to do it at all because contact with other people who were getting help for their problems – and rewards in the form of babies – was so painful. I was ambivalent about the mothers who could, it seemed, conceive so casually and then give their babies away, and scared of the putative and alleged fathers whose perfectly ordinary exteriors hid, I was sure, ravening lust. I still recall the mixture of excitement and fear as I primly invited a very sexy young man to discuss his paternity. That was quite a disturbing experience but I had no way of dealing with it positively; my own life was too complex and I had no supervision – and even if I had, would I have 'told all' to a senior officer?

This subject is so delicate that only by offering something of myself can I really indicate how important I believe it is to know one's own feelings about sexuality (one's own and other people's), to use one's own experiences positively in understanding clients, and to be able to discuss problems and deficiencies in experience in order to gain not personal therapy but clarity, understanding and knowledge. For example, my horror and ignorance severely impaired my ability to work with a family where the father had committed fellatio using his small daughter; I did not even know what fellatio was and was too shy (or was it too stubborn?) to ask.

Religious and moral codes play a very important part too. Doctors may refuse to perform abortions but I am not sure how far social workers are able to be freed from abortion and contraceptive counselling on grounds of principle. Presumably a strongly held principle outweighs most other considerations but I suspect problems arise when the social worker feels dubious about, say, abortion but has not thoroughly examined her feelings.

Problems about sexuality experienced by social workers may be exacerbated by the ambivalent, not to say fearful, attitude of society towards adolescents. Reference has been made in Chapter 3 (pp.

29–30) to legal anomolies and double messages which 'encourage deceit and anxiety, and in many instances involve social workers and others in collusions with young people' (Davis 1980). The double messages of a society which refuses to acknowledge and often punishes the normal, healthy sexuality of its young while countenancing page three of the *Sun* newspaper, *Playboy* and *Esquire* on sale in W.H. Smith, and the existence of 'sex shops', intensify the problems of the social worker.

Working with adolescents, social workers are certain to meet sex whether problematic or not. It may be in some form which has, at the very least, unpleasant aspects, for example incest or VD. It may be a loving relationship between boy and girl intended to last, like that of Denise and Don which, despite (or partly because of) antagonism from the authorities, survived and led to marriage. It may be anxiety because a girl or boy feels unlovely and rejected, unable to attract a boy or girl friend. Or it may be a sexpot, collecting heads and enjoying the power and status.

Of all the emotions which may be excited by working with adolescents and being confronted with matters of sexuality, whether or not as problems, I must mention one more. I have written about possible dislike of a client, but strong attraction is also very possible. I wrote above about the impact on one susceptible young woman of a handsome, provenly-potent man. I imagine that it takes a very controlled male social worker to be immune to the attractions of the young women (or perhaps men) on his caseload. Adolescents do not cease to be sexy just because they are clients. Female social workers too are vulnerable, although perhaps a little less so, unless homosexual, because of the social convention that women are usually attracted by and paired with men of their own age or older. Feeling sexually interested in an adolescent client or knowing oneself to be thus susceptible may cause a social worker to avoid real contact because of fear or even disgust. It may lead to actual sexual encounter which, in my view, would be likely to provoke confusion and trouble for all concerned.

Authority and control

Like it or not, social workers represent authority; they may be employed by the state or a local authority or voluntary organisation; contact with their clients may result from a court order or from a voluntary referral. But whatever the status of and reason for the contact, the social worker is in a *position of authority* and *represents* the authority which employs her. This is an area of great potential difficulty for social workers and has to be worked out both individually and with colleagues.

Rob Grunsell, a teacher, writes on his work in an IT centre:

> I must be continuously aware of how each kid views my authority, whether as duplicate or reverse of their own previous experience of authority figures. Knowing that I must judge how far to accept the mould, how far to insist that I represent something different. To the kid whose experience is of wildly inconsistent authority, I must demonstrate and explain consistency. To the kid whose father has always exercised a violent authority, I must show that authority can be effective without violence, that anger can be controlled on both sides of the relationship. (ND, p. 26)

Rob Grunsell aims to provide the 'consistent, caring controls' without which Howarth and Summers (1978) consider that the adolescent 'will have no means of developing internal ones' illustrated by Lesley whose 'adventures' in care 'ensured that she kept strong external controls while she still needed them', eventually developing 'what looked like very efficient personal control and a sense of her own identity' (Crompton 1978b).

Social workers often feel caught between setting limits and providing external controls – both aspects of authority – and providing their adolescent clients with freedom and respect. Mair Parry describes this dilemma when Sheila, though still in care, goes to live with her boyfriend:

> Should we bring her back to the city and place her yet again in the girls' assessment centre? Having encouraged and enabled her to take responsibility for herself and to make her own decisions, should we now return to the old authoritarian style of care and order her life for her yet again? (1980)

The decision was to support Sheila in her chosen way of life, unlike the authorities who met Denise (15 and a half) and Don on their return to their home town (see p. 33).

Peter Bruggen, a consultant psychiatrist, confronts this kind of problem in his adolescent unit: 'leaning so heavily upon authority and limit setting [it] sometimes seems strange for an open communications system of administration to have developed'. He summarises the cumbersome statement made by the authority to the adolescents living there:

> *We are in charge of this place and we are paid to be so*; we will make the decisions about how it is run but we will welcome your views . . . and sometimes will consult you about them beforehand.
>
> *Your parents (or your social worker if you are the subject of a care*

order) are in charge of where you live and have said that you should be here and for a reason which was stated in your presence.

You are in charge of the rest . . . of your bodies and your minds, or your feelings (. . . pleasant or unpleasant) and ultimately, of course, of your life and whether you live or die. If you have any difficulties with these, we are available to be consulted about them all the time. (Bruggen 1979; my italics)

In contrast John Howells considers that:

For a significant number of field social workers, the removal of the child to a residential setting is far from the 'preferred method of treatment' – it is often seen as explicit *evidence of the failure of their part in the helping process*, and sometimes as enforced handing-over to an agent of social control. By virtue of training or belief, field social workers may not perceive control as a relevant part of the practice with their client . . . *control is confused with authoritarianism and repression*. . . (1978; my italics)

While Peter Bruggen represents the social workers' authority and controlling actions as contributions to a team responsibility, John Howells suggests that social workers are often uneasy about such actions and suspicious of other members of the team whom, he says, they may regard as 'baddies'. I recognise the reluctance to use authority to exercise control, for in my work with Lesley I could think only of keeping her out of the remand home and it was 'With an overwhelming sense of guilt and failure' that I visited her there when at last she was found by the police. I was surprised to discover that she was relaxed and relieved:

I learned from this that my up-till-then unrecognised problem about holding power over, and being in control of, the destiny of another person in fact inhibited my ability to reach into the need of that person and offer what would really be the best service available. I did not wish to seem punitive to Lesley, to risk losing the trust by doing something 'nasty'. Apart from that, *I really did not know whether Lesley feared the remand home and loss of liberty. All I knew, I now realise, was that I feared it, or something like it, for myself.* (Crompton 1978b; new italics)

Writing that article was a great and slightly painful revelation to me, for I did realise my own fears of confinement and difficulties about other people's authority over *me*, being afraid of discomfort, disapproval and punishment and likely to accept the dictates of 'authority'. I was both reluctant to inflict on my clients, and especially the adolescents, things which I feared while at the same time I expected, or rather wanted, them to conform to 'authority' as I did and was confused and distressed when they did not.

In the same article I suggested that

the social worker may set out to establish a friend-to-friend relationship with the adolescent client as a way of avoiding any problem of control; 'I'm one of the boys too you know, identify with me and you'll be OK.' If the social worker is not fully confident of his own adulthood and his own position regarding control (both by and of himself) he may be tempted 'back into adolescence'.   (Crompton 1978b)

Control is achieved not only through use of laws and institutions. Manipulation and labelling are just as effective. If an adolescent does not attend school he may be labelled as a 'truant', a 'school refuser' or a 'school phobic', depending very largely on which service is helping him. He may be received into care; possibly, if he is disruptive, into a CHE. If he shows appropriate signs of disturbance he may be treated at a child or adolescent psychiatric unit where he may easily acquire the label of 'disturbed' or even 'sick'.

Labelling and laziness
This will not be a popular section for I suggest that one source of difficulty for social workers working with adolescents is laziness.

I do not think that social workers are often, if at all, *physically* lazy, although they are often, I think, physically *tired* and this contributes to the kind of laziness I am concerned with here, *moral and mental laziness*. 'Of course', I have heard more often than enough, 'we agree with what you say but we just don't have *time*'; but 'time for social workers and parents and teachers and writers and everyone else is always short. *It is short for children, too*' (Crompton 1980, p. 21; new italics). Time is not a matter solely of the number of working hours between breakfast and bed. It is also what use is made of those hours. Anxiety about departmental reorganisation led my entire team of social workers to huddle over coffee, lunch and tea, which ran into one another (interspersed with grudging attention to clients who telephoned or called, and essential home visits) for several days. Anxiety about work in a particular case can similarly paralyse a worker. This is not laziness but it is an easy step from the paralysis induced by exceptional circumstances to the withdrawal of attention and service to clients occasioned by too much chat. And by 'chat' I do not mean, necessarily, conversation about football and new clothes. A lot of apparently 'professional' conversation is really a device to avoid thinking and doing. (I am not reversing my thoughts about support and consultation, and of course I distinguish between that necessary relaxing social intercourse and time and energy-wasting 'chat'.)

David Brandon and Bill Jordan suggest another way in which social workers inhibit their own working: through self-imposed straight-jacketing. We feel safer (even when resentful) in following the beaten path, avoiding pain and danger and thereby missing opportunities for innovation and adventure. There is ample scope to blame others for our own failure to develop and change. We can blame unresponsive clients, or rigid organizations, or the ignorance of the community for our own complacency and drifting. We can console ourselves that creativity is constantly frustrated by factors beyond our control, preventing us from doing 'real' social work and from realizing our full potential. (Brandon and Jordan 1979, p. 2)

Strong words with which I agree.

One of the easiest ways to be lazy is to accept without question theories of and assumptions about adolescence without really meeting and learning from the individual person. Dorna and her friends hate social workers reading files and forming opinions before meeting the real person. This is particularly manifest and dangerous in *labelling*. For example 'those who break the law . . . are seen and identified as "delinquent" and it is that single identity which largely determines the life-opportunities they have available' (Hugman 1977, p. 15).

Charles O'Brian, an adolescent unit social worker, tells the story of work with Marian 'assessed as being borderline severely sub-normal'. Treatment of Marian was all defined by a 'sticky label' so that the 'real' girl was given no opportunity to emerge. Not surprisingly there were difficulties, and at one point 'as staff anxieties were very high, she was confined to her bed space and sedated'. Progress began only when staff 'had all started looking beyond Marian's label' (O'Brian 1979).

One consequence of defining adolescents by labels and seeing 'everything the client does in terms of symptoms' (Jordan 1970, p. 46) is that the social worker may fail to regard the individual person with *respect*. 'A delinquent', 'a truant', even 'an adolescent' in some part diminishes the individuality of the client, makes it easy to say, '*just* an adolescent' or '*another* delinquent'. So that the kind of laziness I am discussing may lead not only to less progress and help for the adolescent client but even to positive dis-service. Failure to recognise the uniqueness of another person and with this his abilities, strengths and worth, leads to denial of his capability and right to be involved in his own destiny and to take responsibility for himself: 'We rob him of his humanity if we rob him of responsibility' (Bazalgette 1978).

Bill Jordan writes of a case in which he was able to give up 'a false and potentially destructive image of myself as a nice, helpful, understanding and trustworthy person' (1979, p. 91). He risked stepping outside the role which he might have thought his clients expected and which would have been comfortable for himself and, learning about his clients as *individuals*, behaved with them in the way that seemed most useful to them and appropriate to himself.

Fear and violence

On a bus recently I was somewhat overwhelmed by the large and noisy adolescents who crowded on after school. They made no contact with me and I had nothing to fear from them but I did feel some form of fear. And when they had all left the bus I discovered a boy behind me crying. He had been punched by some of the boys, apparently a regular occurrence. I tried to give him some comfort and told him that he should attract the attention of some adult if this happened again. But I wondered what I would have done if I had been called on to intervene and I recognised my own fear of approaching someone known to be physically violent.

Boys in our village have been breaking into and vandalising the closed school building (which we are trying to gain for a desperately-needed community centre). I *think* I understand why the boys do this but I am distressed by their actions and anxious in case I ever have to meet their violence directly instead of by report.

I was lucky to meet very little physical violence as a social worker. My only memory is of a large young adolescent girl who (for a reason which I forget but which did no credit to our skill as social workers) refused to go into a children's home when her mother abandoned the family, and struggled to such an extent that the strongest male child care officer, an ex-policeman, had great trouble in holding her. What a mess we made of it, forcing the girl, through our own fear and ineptitude, to ever-increasing opposition. (Of course she had the choice of not being violent but since it was in her usual pattern of reaction, the odds were well stacked against her suddenly choosing to behave with decorum). I think the worst violence of this incident was in the attitude of the child care officers, which changed from care for a girl in need to a wish to suppress and confine this 'difficult adolescent'.

How much do social workers fear that they may be hurt themselves or fear the menacing violence which may be latent in adolescents? How much do they provoke the violence, possibly physical and frequently verbal, from frustrated clients? Dorna, whom I know as gentle and loving, has described hitting a teacher and being expelled. But the teacher slapped her first and had herself provoked the explosion by verbally pushing Dorna too far.

Social workers may fear their own violence (sympathising, perhaps, with the teacher who slapped Dorna) and the reflection of their controlled but existent feelings in the actions or words of less inhibited adolescents. Or they may reject the idea that some adolescent clients enjoy violence or use it for, say, excitement, material gain, or relief of tension and frustration. Refusing to believe in and face violence may itself help to provoke it.

Some other problems

I have in no way pretended to discuss every hindrance to the development of good work between social worker and adolescent but have suggested some areas of difficulty which may be commonly experienced. The chapter ends with brief notes on a few other possible hindrances.

Confidentiality

Always a potential problem in social worker–client interactions, it may provide an extra irritant for the social worker already struggling to develop a relationship with an adolescent. For example, does a minor have the right to speak to his social worker in confidence or has the social worker a duty to pass on information to his parents? The maintenance of files is also a likely stumbling block: does the adolescent have the right to see his file, or indeed any written material concerning him?

Meeting places

On whose ground should contact take place? Home visits may be undesirable because of lack of privacy – and of the influence of parents even if they are not present. Office interviews may be too official, with the social worker 'protected' by her familiar environment and probably distracted by the telephone and interruptions from colleagues. In coffee bars the social worker may feel conspicuous, as may the adolescent, and street corners can be cold.

Feeling foolish and rejected

It is very easy to feel silly, especially if the social worker thinks that the adolescent is not over-impressed with her. Alongside this is the sensation of rejection. It is really difficult to persevere with attempts to be helpful if one feels unvalued and if those attempts are apparently ignored or turned down. Adolescents who do not co-operate with their social workers can inflict a good deal of pain and dent confidence. They may in turn be rejected.

Anger
For many people, anger is an unacceptable emotion – certainly not to be mixed up with social work. But the frustrations of social work alone are likely to promote anger – and positively used and understood it is not harmful. Robin Hall writes:

> I . . . must confront *my* dilemmas – like anger. I can be forgiven by the boys for being really rather than professionally angry . . . I have come to learn from the children . . . that trust means knowing that your violent feelings are not as destructive as you once feared.   (1979, pp. 28–9)

Sadism
Wilson and Bottomley (1980, p. 20) suggest that the responses of teachers may be influenced by 'unresolved sadism' which can lead to inappropriate and punitive behaviour serving only to exacerbate whatever problems exist with the adolescent pupil (or client).

Giving and receiving warmth and care
A 'difficult challenge is to learn how to express and receive loving feelings without being swallowed up' (Hall 1979, p. 29); but without both giving and receiving love and warmth, social worker and adolescent can expect very stunted and unproductive interaction. Problems sometimes arise from fear of over-involvement, and while collusion is to be avoided, thorough involvement is essential: 'Over-involvement is a possibility only when there is a lack of clarity, identity and self-knowledge in the worker' says Bruce Hugman who, as a detached probation officer, actually lived among his clients (1977, p. 21).

Communication
Finally, for some social workers the paramount problem is feeling that they simply do not know how to communicate with adolescents. They do not know how to talk to them or what to do instead of talking. They feel ignorant of both communication 'techniques' and the technicalities of the appropriate stages of life. They feel so unsure of themselves that they do not know where to start obtaining confidence! I hope that the next chapter will be of help.

5 Adolescents and Social Workers Together

> We all share the same values: honesty and respect for the rights of kids.
> Nothing grandiose, just a fundamental belief in treating kids decently.
> (Leggett 1979, p. 6)

Aims and ideals

The whole person

One of the main messages of this book is that no adolescent, indeed no-one at all, can be helped to change from an unsatisfactory to a satisfying (and I realise that these two words raise a number of questions) way of life if he is only regarded as a symptom or identified by a label. This chapter on helping concentrates on what may happen between the whole individual social worker and the whole individual adolescent. The uniqueness of those giving the service is as important as that of the served.

Ideals

'What is it that these youngsters want and/or need from us?' (Gutridge 1970). 'These youngsters' were the girls in care who attended the group for which Penny Gutridge and a fellow Barnardo's child care officer were responsible. This question is the essential starting point for any work. In this section I introduce the ideas of workers who have really *met* adolescents and tried to answer that question and to offer help and service in the light of the answers.

First let me attempt to counter criticism which is often levelled at books like this – something like 'It's all very well but of course *that's* the *ideal*', implying 'and ideals have nothing to do with reality!'. I believe that the social worker without ideals and the ability to conceive of 'the ideal' for her client is largely wasting her time. 'Whoever', asks Bruce Hugman, writing of experience as a de-tached worker for Sheffield probation service, 'achieved anything but in the pursuit of an ideal?' (1977, p. 2). For him the ideal is 'love . . . the capacity for the rich, caring, joyful relationships . . . especially for those who may have known little enough love, but whose need is above all to love and be loved happily and openly and freely. *Love is not enough, but without it nothing is enough*'

(Hugman 1977, p. 35; my italics). Barbara Kahan, famous in the field of child care for many years, also gives a rallying cry: 'What you do now, affects what happens . . . for 60 or 70 years. Therefore, I bring you back to idealism, to leadership and the importance of considering every child as if it were our own' (1981). Love and leadership – not unreasonable ideals for social workers.

And what are the aims of work born out of such ideals?

Hope

Penny Gutridge saw the girls in her group as 'self-orientated, they have so little to give and thus so little hope of success' (1970). But she worked hopefully. Hope is the great message I received from Audrey, principal social worker in an adolescent psychiatric unit. She told me that she liked working with adolescents because there is 'much more hope than with many other groups'. She sees adolescents as 'people in transition – they aren't going to stay how they are now – tremendously hopeful because on the move' and her work is largely focused on 'trying to help people get hold of their potential and do something with it'. Meeting Audrey was a wonderful experience because she is truly optimistic; she gives the idea of 'transition' a new meaning – a sense of real potential, movement and hope, instead of the patronising and deadening attitudes of some commentators on adolescence. Indeed Audrey finds herself combatting the view of adolescence which gives rise to a 'sense of hopelessness and that this is a terrible time [which] gets over to the family and they worry'. Her aim therefore is to give hope, to support existing strengths, to help the adolescent 'to shift around' and use past experience: 'It's just that you need to shift – you needn't feel as lost as you do – you're doing very well, don't lose heart.'

This aim is reflected in Bruce Hugman's definition of the tasks of social workers, helpers, and educators of all kinds:

> *to stimulate the growth of optimism and courage* in the pursuit of authentic happiness; to help people to free themselves from the impotence and frustration of inappropriate and rigid habits of thought, feeling and behaviour; to assist in the discovery and practice of the means of achieving such ends.   (1977, p. 14; my italics)

Easing the agony and surviving

Penny Gutridge aimed with her group members 'to ease their adolescent agony, an agony just that bit larger than life intended' (1970). Social workers are not usually called in to help people having ordinary experiences in ordinary circumstances; the normal experience of adolescence may bring problems – or extra problems – for the young person in care or with some social, physical or mental disability.

For many adolescents hope may be little known as they desperately try to obtain jobs, pass exams, make relationships, stay out of trouble. Paul McKeever at the Wandsworth Day Care Centre 'had to aim towards survival – for all parties, the parents and siblings as well as the kid' (McKeever 1979, p. 16) and Eddie Leggett, also at Wandsworth, says that, 'for many youngsters, we are trying to hold things together until normal maturation resolves the problems'. His aim was to help the adolescents in trouble survive the period of danger associated with age (for whatever reasons), to 'reduce frequency of criminal activity, or even help prevent it, without embarking on dramatic and expensive expedients' (1979, p. 34).

An adolescent unit social worker told me of work with a 15-year old girl refusing to go to school. The aim of her team was to help the girl improve her ability to relate to people and eventually to obtain and hold down a job. In this case 'survival' was associated with normal maturation since part of the work entailed waiting until the girl was old enough to be employed – and free of the 'threat' of school – for there was no attempt to return her to school, all previous attempts having failed.

Kate Cigno, writing as a senior social worker with a social services department, suggests that the social worker herself may have to do the surviving, if only in terms of waiting alongside the troubled adolescent. Of her work with Mandy, a very storm-tossed girl, she writes, 'I can only now stand by, help her through her mistakes, wait for opportunities to intervene, to "throw back" to her what she is doing so that, maybe, she will learn' (Cigno 1979).

Facing up to reality
Kate Cigno expresses a further aim of work with Mandy: 'getting her to *face up to her reality* (no family to care) while . . . offering her the reassurance that some of us will still be around and interested in her after she reaches the magical age [eighteen]' (my italics).

The unpalatable 'reality' may be external, such as physical deformity or parental rejection; or it may be internal, such as feared aggressiveness or, indeed, softness. Bill Jordan, writing from experience in probation and psychiatric social work, defines the aim: to help the client 'to bear the fear and pain of facing something in himself that he has been trying hard to avoid' (Jordan 1970, p. 56).

A vivid example is given by William Glasser, an American psychiatrist and exponent of reality therapy. This encounter took place in the Ventura School for exceptionally difficult older adolescent girls. Linda, 'who gave us no trouble at the school despite her stormy course in previous institutions' and the psychiatrist

> became involved following our first impromptu lunch table conversation . . . Her first words, stated with mock seriousnesss, were: 'Dr Glasser, I'm here because I'm a very emotionally disturbed girl.' I answered on the same note, 'I can't understand that. Our girls aren't here because they are emotionally disturbed, only because they violated the law. If your only trouble is being emotionally disturbed, I will make it my business to get you out of here because we don't understand anything about complicated psychiatric problems like that.' Then I asked her whether, besides being emotionally disturbed, she happened to do anything that broke the law. She replied, 'I started a riot and slugged a counselor.' This was at a previous school. I said, 'Well, now I understand why you are.' I then shifted my emphasis and asked her with point-blank seriousness, 'Are you going to do that at Ventura?' Probably my direct, honest question reached her because she immediately answered, 'No, I don't think so, I like it here.'   (1975, pp. 114–15)

Responsibility

Facing the reality of one's situation, both the constraints and the possibilities, can be achieved only if one fully accepts responsibility for it. The mixed messages given to our adolescents do not encourage the development of responsibility and interdependence.

Paul McKeever, working with young people referred because of delinquency, encourages them 'to think for themselves, to believe in themselves, and to trust their own perceptions' and endeavours 'to make them aware of their own power and responsibilities; and to strive towards all this in a spirit of mutual help and democracy'. He recognises that 'the main responsibility for a person's behaviour and attitudes rest with the person himself' (McKeever 1979, p. 17–18). Leonard Davis believes that 'we have to begin treating young people as sensible and responsible in their sexual relationships' (1980). Peter said 'If you had more responsibility you'd have more respect.' I interpret this as respect both from other people and for oneself. The development of both, inseparable, kinds of respect is, I strongly believe, one of the prime aims of social work with adolescents.

The helping social worker

That which goes on between people

I am not overlooking the constant and prime importance of material help in many forms of social work with adolescents. But the focus of this book is that which goes on between people, whatever the activity they are engaged in together. The complaints of Dorna, Peter and Jo and Dorna's friends were about how they felt they had been treated, not about material provisions (even though they may have had grounds for dissatisfaction about these as well). They spoke of lack of trust in the professional helpers, feeling that they, the adolescents, could not speak of anything really personal and important; they hated the keeping of files which social workers could see before meeting the individual and they doubted the confidentiality of anything they did say. They felt that most of the helpers showed them little respect and care or paid scant attention to the adolescents' perceptions of their lives and problems. In other words 'that which goes on between people' had not gone on very well. Dorna and Peter might have been found bed and board, but they rarely felt valued or loved.

I have written about social workers and others who work in accordance with their belief in 'honesty and respect for the rights of kids' (Leggett 1979, p. 6), in seeing adolescents as whole, real, individual people. Are such workers of vision and love few and far between? Or were Dorna and Peter and the others just unlucky? Even if social services departments and probation offices and voluntary agencies are overflowing with Bruce Hugmans and Paul McKeevers, Mair Parrys and Audreys, I do not believe we can be content while one Sandra can say, 'I don't trust my social worker.'

But how can a social worker achieve trust? How, against what appear to be considerable odds, can she really make a relationship with an adolescent?

Being trustworthy

First and paramount by being trust*worthy*. And this means being thoroughly clear about her responsibility to and feelings about both the individual adolescent and her employing agency. These may be in conflict; for example the agency may oppose files being read by clients while the social worker may believe that everyone has the right to see everything written about him. Or while the adolescent wants to see his file, the social worker may staunchly, and perhaps unquestioningly, uphold agency policy.

Being trustworthy means too that the adolescent can rely on all actions by and interactions with his social worker being based on consistent concern for his welfare and interest in and respect for his point of view. This does not mean that the social worker always agrees with the adolescent or does just what he wants. (Protection of the adolescent himself or of society or unavailability of material resources may mean that his preferences cannot be met.) But it does mean that the social worker never takes an easy way out nor simply imposes some course of action.

A trustworthy social worker is a whole person in her own right, neither the tool of the agency nor over-identifying with the adolescent himself. The adolescent needs to know who his social worker is – is she real, does she live in the same world as himself? She is bound to have different ideas and experience from him but are these real or 'plastic'?

Trustworthiness also means not being afraid of bad or good experiences and feelings of the adolescent. If he must be disappointed, if he grieves or is angry, or if he is excited or wants to show affection or gratitude, the trustworthy social worker must bear her part. You cannot trust a person who slides out from or resists your emotions. And part of this is always telling the truth with love and often courage.

The trustworthy social worker makes and keeps appointments, and explains truthfully and apologises to the adolescent if she is delayed or prevented. Can you really trust someone who says she will come on Tuesday at five and then does not appear or who promises to call 'sometime'?

Respect

This leads to my next suggestion for relationship-making, *respect*, for one way of demonstrating respect is in showing courtesy in making appointments. Most social workers have suffered from being kept in court waiting rooms for hours on end since their time and convenience are, apparently, of no importance. The time and convenience of adolescents are as important as those of their social workers and a thoughtful approach to making dates can give a very good message; a thoughtless one may very well indicate that this social worker does not respect her clients.

Respect cannot be taught or learned. You can learn respect for behaviour, but not the feeling of respect. It is an easy word to use but not to define. For me it means that all people are unique, experiencing vast ranges of emotions and sensations, forming opinions, holding beliefs, developing ambitions and relationships – in short, living. To respect any other person I should approach him always with courtesy, consideration for his need and right to feel whole and valued, never assuming that, perhaps because I do not like him or we hold differing views, he is wrong, but never afraid to let him know if I disagree with him. Respect precludes that patronising attitude which under the guise of 'protection' sometimes assumes that other people less 'strong' or 'well-adjusted' than the speaker cannot bear truth and reality. (I realise that 'truth' and 'reality' are not absolutes but cannot here engage with that large debate. It is, however, important for social workers to know their own definitions of and attitudes towards these tricky matters.)

Respect is very often lacking in work with adolescents. Young people who come to the attention of social workers may have plenty of experience of not being respected, by teachers, parents, maybe residential staff and police, possibly other social workers. Recall Sheila, turned down by the careers officer because of her tattoos and Denise, plunged back into the children's home because she had not reached the suitable age for living with Don. The social worker has a vital opportunity to repair this damage and through showing the adolescent respect to earn it herself. If you have never felt respected, can you feel and show it (as opposed to obsequiousness) to anyone else? And if you do not respect anyone else can you really feel it (as opposed to pride and self-righteousness) for yourself?

Really respecting an adolescent would make it impossible not to show him his file, involve him in reviews, ask for his contribution to court reports, and so on. Linda Hill, working in a local authority young people's counselling project, believes that she is

> seen as independent from teachers, parents and social workers by the young people I see, and I know many are greatly reassured when I tell them that anything they say to me is in confidence. I never contact other agencies behind people's backs; even when I make a referral, the young person will always be there while I'm on the telephone. Any case notes I make (and these are kept to a minimum) are available for the young person to see. (Hill 1980, p. 10)

Respect for the decisions of an adolescent may be very difficult either to feel or to enact. How easy they may be to discount because the adolescent does not understand the problem, lack of resources, general impracticability and apparently inevitable doom of his plan! Lynda, a probation officer, told me of a remarkable court which did respect the decision of a 15-year old boy, despite the reservations of both court and probation officer. 'Kevin' was living with his father pending the hearing of his mother's application for custody (which court and probation officer favoured). Although fully aware of the difficulties and discomforts of remaining with his father and, Lynda suspected, very probably preferring his mother, Kevin threatened to run away, truant, even commit suicide if removed from his father. The court respected the strength of Kevin's feelings and adjourned the hearing for a trial period. In this time, against all expectations, Kevin did very well and custody was eventually granted to his father. The motives for Kevin's decision are not important in this particular discussion; the importance is in the willingness of probation officer and court to take a risk, backing the clear and strong decision of the boy against what might have seemed like better sense.

Taking a risk, or not preventing an adolescent from taking one, is good evidence of trust and respect. Mair Parry demonstrates this in her account of work with Sheila. After many troubles and the tragedy of a miscarriage (Sheila and her boyfriend had welcomed the pregnancy) Sheila found losing her baby

> the end of a long line of rejection and disappointment.
> She signed herself out of hospital and was again staying at a friend's flat. Her health deteriorated to the point of extreme concern. I saw her and spoke with her. The conflict between allowing Sheila to make her own decisions and doing nothing while she destroyed herself became almost unbearable for me personally. But the first principle of my work with Sheila had been trust and cooperation; I could not at this stage take 'unilateral' control again. Instead, I told her that I was concerned about her, that I cared, and I explored with her the possibilities open to her.   (Parry 1980)

Shortly after this Sheila herself asked for a foster home, able to accept at least temporary care because, I suppose, she felt in control herself rather than controlled by her social worker. This was surely a great endorsement of both the care and the respect given by Mair Parry who records that when she first met Sheila 'she was tired of having her life directed by social workers and being made to feel that everyone just wanted to get rid of her'. This recalls Dorna who absconded from the secure unit of her CHE largely to show she could do it but in the 'house' 'abided by the rules. We did them of our own free will. Never once were we ordered to do something. And because of this we didn't mind doing it.'

Love
However trustworthy and respecting the social worker I think her relationships will be lacking if they are not also based on love. By this I mean not a sentimental sympathy for the deprived or affection for some favourite but a love which transcends irritation and frustration, fear and attraction, the love which really cares. No pile

of words can explain this; if you feel it, you know, and you know too if colleagues work through and out of love.

I called a chapter of *Respecting Children* 'Not by Treatment but by Love', quoting an annual report of the Northorpe Hall Trust (NHT), an IT centre in Yorkshire. 'At Northorpe we try to heal the wounds between adults and the children, not by "treatment", but by love' (NHT 1978). The love at Northorpe Hall provides that there is a firm structure, the security of external controls and objectives individually tailored to each boy.

> Whatever the *doing* at Northorpe Hall the *being* is all about believing that the boys are all important worthwhile people, for there is no such thing as an unimportant worthless person. The boys may have committed offences, they may believe those around them who persistently tell them that they are rubbish, they may think that love is nothing but a word in girls' comics; at Northorpe Hall they meet respect, concern and love without sentimentality or collusion, 'stern love'. (Crompton 1980, p. 216)

It was surely 'stern love' which Dorna and her colleagues showed to Gemma when they showed her how much they cared by kicking her all over (see p. 3). Through that 'bit of love' Gemma regained 'her sense of self-respect'. Gemma's response to this treatment shows that she was quite able to understand the message of love which the kicks gave. Although social workers cannot use this form of communication, the story is still a good parable. Love and the exercise of authority are not by any means mutually exclusive. Mair Parry, painfully standing by while Sheila was in danger of 'destroying herself' was not refusing the 'care and control' part of her responsibility; but she was choosing with a particular girl to express her loving in a particular way. With Lesley I had to learn that loving for that particular girl was best expressed by exercising maximum external control, an experience of loving which, like Mair Parry's, entailed considerable pain (Crompton 1978b).

Love does mean trying really to know the loved person, reaching out from one's own needs, fears and satisfactions to that other person. Dorna's friend Sandra gives deeply-felt advice from long experience of social workers:

> don't be frightened to get involved with the kids cos the more involved you are the more they respect you. Also *give them a lot of love and attention* and they'll tell you all you want to know (all their problems). Half of them suffer from neglect and *all they need is someone to love them*.   (see p. 6; my italics)

Some social workers regard attention as rather a low level need:

'he's only attention-seeking' or 'he likes a lot of attention' really separate the client's perfectly normal needs from those of the rest of us. One social worker who spoke of a client like that went on to talk of her own enjoyment of amateur dramatics where, presumably, she also liked the attention. (And what could be more attention-seeking than writing a book?)

When attention is joined with love a great deal may be achieved as in the story of Dorna's care for Karen born of 'a kind of love which you only experience in a home . . . To experience this was unbelievable because it seemed to catch on to the staff' (see p. 4). Perhaps the staff felt this kind of love anyway; if not, it is reassuring that they seemed to catch on. But it is far from reassuring that 'her social worker had no faith in her'. Why not?

A personal view

I asked a number of people in social work what they thought social workers could do and how they could help adolescents. Emily Engel wrote to me:

> What can social workers do? Be honest, unprejudiced, and abstain from the sarcasm which characterises much interaction between adolescents and their 'carers' – an irritating, offensive and unfair defensive tactic which is often passed off as fun.
>
> How can/do we help? With tolerance, fairness and honesty – by being 'good examples' of creative, realistic, interested adults as well as being helpful and supportive. Consistency and confidence are, I think, the most essential personal characteristics for people who want to work closely with adolescents, after interest and liking of course!

Communicating

Many people, however much they feel love and respect for their adolescent clients, find developing and working within relationships very difficult because they feel that they do not know how to communicate. There is perhaps a spectre of a totally uncommunicative or massively aggressive adolescent, utterly refusing to respond to the well-intentioned overtures of the would-be helpful social worker.

In my own experience of working with adolescents and, later, of enjoying friendships, I have never met the bogies of such fantasies. I was far from being the best-ever social worker and I certainly did not achieve all my goals with my adolescent clients. Perhaps those girls and boys, now men and women, would add their criticisms of me to those of Dorna and her friends about their social workers. But I did not find them unapproachable or rejecting; the main obstacle to good communication was my own lack of confidence.

As this is not a book about how to communicate I can offer only a few practical suggestions but I hope that these will aid confidence and stimulate further ideas.

Listening and waiting

It is impossible really to learn about another person if you do all the talking and doing. Both Jo and Dorna said that social workers 'should listen more' and the comments of Peter and Dorna's friends suggest that all too often the conversation with social workers was confined to questions and criticisms. How often do social workers seem to have visited only 'when you're in trouble. When you're good nobody remembers but when you're bad nobody forgets' Mark, p. 7)?

David's view of a 'good social workers' is that 'you have to be a good listener with a sympathetic nature and most of all you have to be able to advise the kids in the best way fit' (see p. 5). But in order to give appropriate advice in a way which enables it to be used, the listening must have been real *listening* – as opposed to just not speaking or vaguely hearing.

Paul, a senior social worker in a social services department, told me how he had received a great gift from a boy, the gift of confidence because he 'listened'. 'Neil' had been a member of a small group run by Paul as a social worker within the withdrawal unit of a comprehensive school. The aim of the group was to discuss the members' own views of their 'problems' and whether or not these related to the views of social workers, parents and teachers. Much of Paul's work was 'unscrambling messages' between, for example, the pupils and the unit staff teachers – 'he says you said "no" but what *did* you say'? So much trouble arises from people *thinking* they have said or understood something which has been misunderstood or not intended by the other person.

Neil certainly found Paul's clarity and ability to listen very helpful. One day he asked Paul (who was not his own social worker) what he would say if he, Neil, admitted some criminal offences. Paul answered 'I'd have to tell the police.' Neil did confess his crimes and then with Paul's aid decided how to tell the police himself. When Neil was ready Paul accompanied him to the police station. Here Paul himself did the talking, Neil correcting him. This, Paul says, helped Neil learn how to communicate with the police, easing the difficulty of actually making the confession. One important point in this story is that Paul had been prepared *not* to listen – not to receive

Neil's confidences if Neil did not wish the police to be told. But when he did listen, he listened well. And indeed he listened well to Neil's first approach, 'What would you say if . . .?' He *heard* that Neil wanted to give the information and, knowing the boy, he could assess correctly that help to go to the police would be a good outcome for Neil. (Social workers do not always consider that they must report the crimes of their clients to the police; a complicated and important topic which cannot be discussed here.)

Two years after this incident and after the sequence of group meetings Paul and Neil met again and Neil asked Paul to be his social worker 'because you listened'. He also told Paul that he had confessed because he felt safe; although he knew he would have to go to the police and was in that way very far from safe, he believed that *Paul* would not condemn him. And yet he had not felt safe to tell his own social worker.

Listening may not be to the words of another person. It may mean attending to their actions or to the words behind the words. Connie Benton, a social services department social worker, really listened to Jane, a 14-year old 'who had periodically refused to attend school from the age of seven'. Following a long line of would-be helpers, Connie Benton found many ways of listening to and waiting for Jane, realising that for 'this timid child an extremely gentle approach was required'. But one day when

> I was having a hectic time with other cases . . . I asked Jane if she could meet me at the civic centre, she agreed but then failed to arrive. On enquiry, I discovered that she had arrived at reception but had panicked at using the lift to my office on the eighth floor. I was angry with myself at my lack of thought. (Benton 1979)

Not angry with Jane for causing inconvenience; Connie Benton 'listened' to what had happened and recognised that the task had been too great for Jane, the 'timid child', who had achieved a great deal in reaching the civic centre at all. The sequel was that 'I called on Jane at home later that morning', not leaving the girl to worry about her failure to keep an appointment but straightaway showing that nothing, including her social worker's goodwill, was lost.

Patricia Goldacre, a teacher in a school for maladjusted children, understands very well the value of waiting. Thirteen-year old Teddy 'never came into the classroom without a broom handle or pole in his hand with which he was ready to attack us (defend himself)'. On one particular morning Teddy would not settle and became increasingly distracted. Eventually 'he said, "Right, you've all had it. I'm going to wreck this place." I said, "What's the matter, Teddy?"

and he said "Fuck off you and shut your mouth." ' Patricia Goldacre 'decided to sit through his rage calmly, commenting when it
might restrain him, and watch.' The alternative was probably 'a
stand up fight with him' with or without 'reinforcements'. Teddy
went to work.

> If I did not watch he would throw the books at me till I did, I knew. He
> hurled the books off my table. He ripped a calendar off the wall. He
> threw some books across the room. He threw some sheets of painting
> paper onto the floor, hurled two paper towel rools across the room and
> dripped black paint over the easel. Respecting Teddy's need to show his
> feelings, the other children went on working with their heads down. I
> watched Teddy gravely. He was grinding his teeth and I was careful not
> to grind mine. *I knew how empathetic he would be with any hint of anger*
> *and tension on my part.*

Eventually Teddy said ' "I'm not going to clear this up, you know,"
thereby letting me know that his rage was abating and that he
thought he should.' Even better was to come.

> He looked at a doll's dress which we had just finished making and he
> said, 'No, I won't destroy that, it's too good.' *That was the most hopeful*
> *thing I had heard him ever say*. He was showing . . . that he was able to
> express his feelings, to exert control over his actions and that he saw
> some good things in the world after all.

Soon after this Teddy 'tipped his desk over quite gently as a final
gesture and went out of the classroom to kick a ball in the yard'
(Goldacre 1979; all italics mine).

Patricia Goldacre showed considerable nerve in waiting for the
hurricane to pass. But she also showed a good understanding of
Teddy and the will to help him. Had she fought him, alone or with
colleagues, everyone would have lost and the battle would have
been rejoined another day. By waiting for him and surviving his
anger she enabled Teddy to see 'some good things in the world after
all.' This kind of understanding and waiting helped Teddy to avoid
the dire future which some people foresaw for him: 'Everyone
said I'd be in detention centre or borstal by the time I was 18, but
here I am 18 and you see I'm not.'

Of course physical restraint may sometimes be the right course.
As ever the vital factor is being so attentive to the needs, behaviour
and messages of the individual child at the particular time that
the social worker can assess, quickly, even intuitively, the most
appropriate response.

Words
I suppose the most obvious means of communication for social

workers is speech and to illustrate the use of conversation with adolescents I have chosen an article by Judy Stevenson, writing of experience in a social services department. The article is mainly an account of a day spent with Jacob and Noah, aged about 16, in the waiting room – and eventually the court room – of a juvenile court. The day starts at 9 a.m. when Judy Stevenson collects the boys from an assessment centre and finishes sometime after 6 p.m. when Jacob is driven away in a police car. The wait for hearing lasts from 10 a.m. till after 4.30 p.m.

Through the article Judy Stevenson, Jacob and Noah become vividly alive, passing through numerous moods. For example, in the car:

> 'I want a 1961 penny', said Noah, 'that is the year I was born, and it must be worth money before I am dead.' He sang a song about a girl, saying he would never let her down. On the way, a green car passed us, with two white men in front, and a black girl on the back seat. 'She must be going to court', said Jacob. 'I thought of that', I said, 'but perhaps she's an ambassador's daughter.'
>
> And all the time, Jacob and I were wondering if he would go to Borstal.

In the waiting room:

> 'Pray to God', said Noah, 'that tonight I'll be at my front door, free to walk the streets.'
> 'Dreams', I said, and the boys nodded their heads.
> 'We all need dreams', and they nodded again wisely.
> 'But the thing is to know when they are dreams.'

Much much later, after lunch in a Wimpey bar, a game of rummy and Jacob slowly reading his court report:

> 'Do you think what I've said is fair?' I asked. He wouldn't comment.
> 'What's she recommending?' asked Noah.
> 'What am I recommending?' I asked Jacob.
> 'She's leaving it to the court' he said.

(This had already been discussed with Jacob on a previous day so the idea was not sprung on him but he was, clearly and naturally, very anxious.) Later still:

> 'How is it', said Noah's social worker, pulling up Jacob's trouser leg, 'that you are wearing a lovely pair of socks and smart shoes, when Noah is wearing no socks, and these awful old shoes?'
> 'They're the best socks in the world', said Noah.
> 'I bought them', said Jacob.
> 'Yes, you did buy them', I said to Jacob, 'and you bought that jacket, didn't you? You know where you got the money to buy them.' 'Yes', he said.

'Where did you get your fingers?' Jacob asked Noah.
'I got this one in Woolworths, and these three in Timothy Whites. This one in Cecil Gees, and these five', he said, 'I got them in Harrods.'

Throughout all the conversations Judy Stevenson is aware of the anxiety of Jacob, his longing for a miracle to save him from borstal, his need to keep his self-respect in the court room. She can join in the humorous exchanges, meet Jacob's pleas with honesty, respond to him as a person with whom she has a special relationship.

Touch
But the end of the account is not about words. It is about another important and, by social workers, little-used means of communication: 'When I *touched* him through the window of the police car, before they drove him to Latchmere House, to say goodbye and tell him I would come and see him, he was crying' (Stevenson 1979; my italics).

When I tried to read that to my husband, I was crying too.

There are many occasions when a comforting arm can do more than the most exquisite words but when I was reading widely in preparation for *Respecting Children* I found that 'It may have been the accident of my choice of literature and live sources but I have not been overwhelmed with examples of social workers deliberately using physical contact to aid communication with their child clients' (Crompton 1980, p. 174). My further reading for this book has produced only Judy Stevenson's touch on Jacob's arm. I feel justified, therefore, in referring to my own chapter 'Keep In Touch' which includes another story from William Glasser who tells of his help to the teacher of a very difficult, large and abusive epileptic mentally retarded boy. The teacher was rejecting the boy and said that he was far too busy for any personal counselling. William Glasser writes:

> I asked him if he could devote ten seconds twice a day to the boy to start a program, a request so limited that he could not refuse. I suggested that he put his arm around the boy's shoulder each day when he entered and when he left class, saying that he was glad to have the boy in class and asking whether he could help him to do the work ... Following my suggestion for one week, the teacher reported a remarkable change. The boy was pleasant, and his aggressive, abusive behaviour had almost stopped. A total investment of about two minutes had started the involvement and had begun the behavior change. (Glasser 1975, p. 198)

Some social workers may find it natural to offer a simple handshake which provides physical and usually eye contact.

Earlier in 'Keep In Touch', I refer to the possible dangers of touching clients and perhaps in particular adolescents, for social workers are very vulnerable both to accusations of sexual assault and to misunderstanding – an apparently simple non-sexual arm-round-shoulder may be understood as a sexual invitation. But

> if it really would be unwise and dangerous for the social worker herself to supply the hugging she must ensure that someone will be ready to offer cuddles for comfort. In saying this I am not forgetting that sometimes unhappy people of whatever age cannot tolerate physical contact . . . part of the skill of cuddling is knowing when to sit quietly, untouching and when to slip the kind arm around the sad shoulder.   (Crompton 1980, pp. 175–6)

One of the most satisfactory ways for social workers to share physical contact and care for adolescents might be through sport, for example swimming or rough-and-tumble football.

> Few active games can be played without physical contact and many social workers know the value of a game of football with the opportunity for hugging and horse-play with otherwise too-big-to-cuddle boys and of an hour in the swimming baths where inhibitions may be shed with clothes and social workers may offer comfort to tense children by supporting them in the water, suggesting by their strength and ability to keep their physical heads above water that they may be trustworthy and even able to save emotional heads from drowning.   (Crompton 1980, p. 183)

Places

The contacts described in the section on touch took place in car and waiting room, football pitch and swimming pool – anywhere but sitting down in an office.

Connie Benton took the timid school-refusing Jane on a number of outings:

> The initial outing had been a nerve-racking experience for her, she was so much like a frightened bird, one wrong move and she might have flown off. Her first attempt to get into my car was an ordeal, with great hesitancy in opening the door and an attitude of timidity during the drive. Very gradually, I got to know and better understand her fears and her feelings, her interests and abilities. Beyond this I began to get through to her emotional needs, phobias and endeavoured to find the root cause for these.   (Benton 1979)

Paul could not take the members of his school group out in a car but he did whenever possible leave the classroom for the school field. Here the members could stroll off, leaving the group for a while or staying on the edge, and all felt more comfortable about adopting postures not perhaps commonly seen in classrooms, such as lying on the floor. He found that free and relaxed positions, plus space, were very helpful to communication.

Where you try to communicate is an essential part of the communication itself. Jo was interviewed in the psychiatrist's office – where he was at home and she was not; Dr X does not seem to have made much effort, or at least not much effective effort, to help Jo feel at ease there. If much contact with adolescents must take place within offices I wonder whether social workers are concerned about the probable effects of this on their interactions and relationships. The social worker who 'owns' office, desk, means of making tea and telephone (which may demand attention at any moment) is in a very powerful position.

Working within the adolescent's home may be difficult too, for the actual or felt presence and power of parents may be very inhibiting to both adolescent and social worker. 'Home' means wherever the adolescent lives, for I painfully remember a house parent sitting at the end of the room weeping while I as social worker, shyly and in increasing embarrassment, talked with some girls. This is perhaps rather an extreme example, but it made me conscious of the intricacies of interaction. I believed in spending time alone with my young clients but did not know how to achieve this gracefully within the web of relationships, feelings and anxieties within the home.

David West, a probation officer, writes about the problem of place and his solutions:

> I supervised a 17-year old youth who had been placed on probation and who was resentful of authority. He would not communicate and our interviews in the office were laboured. He was not keen for me to visit his home because he saw himself as the male authoritarian figure in the household in the absence of his father, and when I did visit his home, my presence created discomfort for both him and his mother . . .
> Eventually, I took [him] across the road from the office through a local park on foot, to a cafe where we drank some coffee. Quite suddenly he began to talk about himself, his family and his strong feelings about his absent father, his philosophy of life and his anxieties and aspirations.
> (West 1979)

Useful contact could begin.

Most social workers have the energy to walk across the road to a café and lift a coffee cup but perhaps not all could use David West's device of 'a chat before and after a jog around a running track'. *Before*, maybe! My own preference was for walking in the park or country when the pressure to keep up conversation is so much less than sitting in a confined space consciously 'interviewing'.

Lynda, the probation officer, told me how a student had taken a girl to an exhibition and learned a great deal (about the subject of the exhibition, the girl herself and communication, I imagine) and she commented 'maybe we're not imaginative enough – maybe there *is* time' – for one of the common complaints of social workers is about lack of time. But time wasted is time thrown away, while a few extra hours given to real communication may save much time eventually.

Meeting in a group

Penny Gutridge and her colleague were certainly imaginative when they offered informal meetings to the 'half a dozen or so' girls, rejected from a variety of foster and other homes, who lived in a special foster home. The group, convened for one particular meeting, grew and flourished. The stimulus had been a suspected pregnancy and

> the ensuing excitement and debate revealed some very weird distortions of factual knowledge as well as some gruesome suggested remedies for the predicament, plus a total inability to use the problem in any sort of context. An engineered opportunity for informal discussion seemed indicated.

This led to weekly meetings on more neutral territory at the home of a more senior child care officer. Focus was on education about 'begetting children, providing a home and family structure, the moral and practical issues involved, inter-relationships, and the plain physical care of babies and children'. Experts from various fields (for example a midwife) helped and a television series 'Having A Baby' was watched 'religiously'.

> Sessions tended to be protracted long into the night with talk swinging from the general to the particular as the night wore on. Individuals began to talk about their own past, their history and parentage, the whys and wherefores etc. Even the least articulate participated . . . sometimes one or other CCO [was] monopolised by a particular youngster almost to the point of being devoured as the intensity of her thoughts demanded some form of concentrated verbal expression and hence attention.

This is particularly important, for no amount of group activity and interaction can supercede one-to-one contact and much of the value of Penny Gutridge's group was in the facilitation of individual conversations: 'The kitchen became a haven of privacy for some. "I want to talk to you." "I've been thinking–." ' I imagine that many social workers would give their ears to hear 'I want to talk to you' (Gutridge 1970).

Companionable quiet

In contrast, sometimes the best service a social worker can give is to offer the chance to be quiet – no talk, no discussion, no shared activities, just companionable quiet. The pressured life of many adolescents gives little opportunity for stopping and reflecting. An adolescent in some sort of trouble may not need anything more than a release from pressure, some time and space to sit still inside himself and just get straight. Perhaps that was what Jo most needed, together with reassurance that she was 'normal'. Few people are good at offering quietness and social workers also feel under pressure to be seen as *doing*. The peaceful presence of a social worker for an hour can offer protection from other people who would break up the adolescent's quiet, can communicate its own peacefulness, can receive anything the adolescent may feel like saying.

Writing

A silent occupation which may lead to spoken communication or may be forever private is writing. Connie Benton records that she 'encouraged' Jane 'to write a daily diary' (Benton 1979). Jane seems to have kept her diary to herself but Sheila read to Mair Parry

> from a diary that she had kept intermittently for several years. It was full of accounts of past experiences, bitter feelings about her parents and those people who had been responsible for her in care. Sheila revealed a very deep feeling that she wanted to be loved unreservedly for herself – she wanted a family. (1980)

Jo, writing some notes for this book two years after her experience with Dr X, said: 'I have added a few things which I feel I didn't explain fully when we talked together, or indeed, which I hadn't tried to analyse in my mind before then, and have only now sorted out *in words* as being what I did/do feel.'

Fun

I wrote briefly at the end of Chapter 3 about fun and it would be wrong to discuss communication with adolescents without some further reference, for social work without fun, or at least some lightness and a sense of humour, is not likely to reach 'the whole' adolescent. Penny Gutridge's group preceded discussion of abortion, VD and so on with records and 'youngsters in a crazy conglomeration of gear, lounging or jogging rhythmically in a haze of ciggy smoke and amidst a litter of coffee cups' (1970). Noah and Jacob managed some marvellous verbal fun with Judy Stevenson on the way to court; at the beginning of that trying day Noah even sang. I have never been very good at 'fun' myself and I think my relationships with adolescents might have been easier if I had had a lighter touch. 'The vitality of the young people' (Robinson 1981) is expressed so much through 'a crazy conglomeration of gear', through movement, music and humour, and if the social worker has no contact with this she has not really *met* the individual adolescent.

Plans and contracts
The focus of social work help is largely determined by the reason for contact between social worker and adolescent and the responsibilities and functions of the social work agency. 'That which goes on between people' has to go on within some structure. This section is a brief look at some aspects of the structure of social work with adolescents.

Contracts
Although confusion is essential to the plots of opera and P.G. Wodehouse it may have very serious results in everyday life. Not the least of the adolescent's confusions is very probably about just why he is expected to have anything to do with a social worker and what he is supposed to do. Considering how difficult it is for many (most?) social workers clearly to express understanding of their work it is not surprising if clients find this obscure.

One purpose of working with adolescents must be to reduce confusion and the work itself must provide *an experience of clarity*, not of confusion. A useful device to aid this is the making and keeping of a contract between social worker and adolescent. Much of the experience of children and adolescents is being told what to do or not to do. A contract involves the adolescent in making a decision about what is to be aimed at, what definitely achieved.

Eddie Leggett and his colleagues thought it important 'to clarify exactly where both parties stood' (IT and children). Verbal contracts were preferred 'because the children were generally suspicious of written documents, especially when their reading ability was fairly low. Also the verbal contract allowed far greater flexibility in negotiations for any subsequent modification or change.'

Everyone likely to be concerned in the particular 'kind of service to be offered' became party to the contract. Its purpose is clearly stated:

> What this process did was to place the responsibility on the workers to make it clear to the child who they were and why they were offering help.

It gave an opportunity for the child to assess what he or she was being invited to do and a chance to accept or reject it. Once accepted and agreed, the contract became a major reference point for future inter-action and acted as a reminder to both parties of the reasons for being together and what the obligations were on both sides. *We believe that contracts are a good start in the development of relationships which reflect our basic aspirations of respect for, and honesty with, each other*.

(Leggett 1979, p. 7; my italics)

An excellent description of working within just such a contract is given by Marian Liebmann in her article about Phil, an 18-year old attending a voluntary day centre for ex-offenders and other adults with problems, run under the aegis of Gloucestershire probation and after-care committee. The article traces Phil's progress by means of a number of contracts. Phil chose to make his first contract with Sue, a student on a six-month placement.

Why I want to become a member: In the past I have had difficulty in getting to know people and I still am a 'loner'. I want to learn to trust people and make friends and improve myself. How:

Learning to trust people by: making an effort to mix with people in the lounge; getting involved with others in the centre activities; coming to the social club every Wednesday evening.

Improving myself by: improving my reading – lessons with Ernie at 9.45 on Wednesdays and Fridays; work simulation project every Tuesday; to use the workshop at any other times.   Phil/Sue

A great deal of help and improvement followed but eventually, for various reasons, further troubles came to Phil and he stayed away from the centre. On his return a new contract was drawn up, this time with Marian (since Sue had left). It focused on preparation for his sister's wedding and 'his writing had improved considerably so he wrote this one himself, letter by letter'. Aims included making 'a coffee table for a wedding present for my sister' and saving money to hire a suit.

The story continues through several more contracts which Phil fulfilled with various degrees of success. Marian Liebmann con-cludes: 'He has certainly achieved something through his contracts, but were they just a structured interlude in a confused and direc-tionless life? As in all social work, we shall have to wait and see' (Liebmann 1980).

Unlike those of the Wandsworth workers, the contracts of Marian Liebmann and her colleagues do not seem to have specified the undertakings of the staff members. This is important, for the adolescent should have the opportunity to review the social worker's progress with and fidelity to *her* part of the agreement.

Roles and tasks of the social worker

Earlier in this chapter, I discussed some of the aims which the social worker may have for and with her adolescent clients. But achievement of such aims depends in part on the social worker's understanding of her contributions not only in terms of *being* (trustworthy, respecting, loving) and *communicating* but also through the official focus of her contact.

The social worker may, for example, be responsible to a court and bound therefore to include her relationship with the court in any contract. A supervision or probation order would include requirements to return to court if the adolescent failed to honour the order. Preparation of a report to a court would entail explaining to the adolescent that information about him would have to be collected from various sources (including of course himself).

As important as information-getting is information-giving. There is nothing like mystery to increase anxiety. A court appearance, an operation, a move, all are likely to be more manageable if the adolescent has been given information and the chance to ask questions. The social worker may also need to give information about, for example, the whereabouts of parents and other family members. A third kind of information is 'hard fact', for example about legal and welfare rights and educational, leisure and job opportunities.

For this kind of information the social worker may take on another role, helping the adolescent to contact such appropriate agencies as Citizens' Advice Bureaux, local authority education departments and employment offices.

Since communication with other officers and officials is sometimes difficult the social worker is often an escort and enabler, like Paul helping Neil make his confession to the police. She may also be a buffer and interpreter between, for example, the adolescent and his parents or care staff.

The social worker may herself hold parental responsibility on behalf of the local authority which entails, among other things, home-finding and supervision.

Planning

Unless the social worker's contact with her adolescent client is very brief it is almost bound to involve planning, making and implementing decisions. The focus of the plan may be the recommendation to a matrimonial court regarding custody of an adolescent; or to a juvenile court regarding a care or supervision order. It may be a move from children's home to foster home or from foster home to natural parents. It may be investigation of proposed abortion or adoption or preparation for death from some disease. Whatever the focus, whatever the social worker's preference, a plan can only be really useful to an adolescent if it is made *with* him. More often than not the range of possibilities is limited, and planning must include ensuring that the adolescent recognises this. But also the social worker must pay thorough attention to the opinions and feelings of the adolescent and be alert to the possibility that *his* plan, despite apparent constraints and difficulties, may work, especially if it is what he really wants to do.

'We are ourselves'

In this wide-ranging chapter I have suggested some aims and ideals for working with adolescents, some qualities which I consider essential for the social worker, some ways of communicating and some points about planning. This is certainly a quart in a pint pot and that quart is only a sample from a wide sea.

To close the chapter and the book I have chosen extracts from a novel and an autobiography, for I believe with Bruce Hugman that 'training to be of use to others should have . . . to do with poets and novelists, and the great sensibilities of the past and present' (1977, p. 2). First a conversation between a 17-year old girl (shocked and grieving at the sudden news that her father is to remarry, introducing into a settled and happy home a woman whom she dislikes) and a slightly older young man, her self-appointed 'social worker'.

'It is difficult,' he went on, 'but by-and-by you will be so much happier for it.'

'No I shan't', said Molly, shaking her head. *'It will be very dull when I shall have killed myself, as it were, and live only in trying to do, and to be, as other people like. I don't see any end to it. I might as well never have lived. As for the happiness you speak of, I shall never be happy again.'*

There was an unconscious depth in what she said, that Roger did not know how to answer at the moment; it was easier to address himself to the assertion of the girl of seventeen, that she should never be happy again.

'Nonsense; perhaps in ten years' time you will be looking back on this trial as a very light one – who knows?' 'I daresay it seems foolish; perhaps all our earthly trials will appear foolish to us after a while; perhaps they seem so now to angels. *But we are ourselves, you know, and this is now*, not some time to come, a long, long way off. And we are not angels to be comforted by seeing the ends for which everything is sent.' (Gaskell 1969 [1864–6], p. 170; my italics)

All adolescents are *themselves* and their *now* is what counts, for the

60 or 70 years' future of Barbara Kahan's concern starts *now*. We must ensure that social work is not a device for helping adolescents to 'live only in trying to do, and to be, as other people like'.

Despite adversity Molly was to live happy ever after but Jimmy Boyle's chequered adolescence in the 1950s has led to his residence in Barlinnie Prison serving a life sentence for murder. He must have seemed the typical folk devil, uncontrolled and uncontrollable adolescent, yet of his feelings about life in an approved school he writes:

> The ordinary staff in the school were very much like those that I had met in schools outside and there was always this feeling of distance between us. During my whole period in St John's I never got close to any of them even to talk to on a superficial basis as all of us kept our distance. There were barriers there and the only one ever to penetrate these barriers was the head man, Brother Paul. He was an admirable person, one who was interested and who cared. He was the one man who made any impression on me, who wasn't afraid to get to know the kids or to give a part of himself to us. He did strange things to all of us with the relationships he tried to build with everyone. He made us all feel very guilty about doing things that were wrong. It's not that he had the chance to get to know any of us really well as he seemed always to be swamped in administrative duties but when he was about and when he spoke, his actions made every one of us pay attention. He cut through all the phoneyness and we were able to see that he was the genuine article. His presence was a luxury, but the unfortunate thing was that he was the only one with this attitude and sensing this he would take progressive steps to include us by discussing things, such as the money that was allocated to him each year. He would inform us as to how it would be spent and ask for opinions. The fact that he brought us into it even though we didn't always understand, gave us some sense of responsibility . . .   (Boyle 1977, pp. 72–3)

For Jimmy Boyle, Brother Paul's presence was a luxury. But Brother Paul represents the attitudes and qualities to which every adolescent in trouble has a right.

Bibliography

ND = no date given

Bazalgette, J. 1978, 'The policeman within', *Journal of Adolescence*, vol.1, no.1, pp.89–95

Benton, C. 1979, 'Social work in action: school refusal – whose problem?' *Social Work Today*, vol.10, no.18, pp.16–17

Boyle, J. 1977, *A Sense of Freedom*, London, Pan Books (first published by Canongate Publishing Ltd., Edinburgh)

Brake, M. 1980, *The Sociology of Youth Culture and Subcultures*, London, Routledge & Kegan Paul

Brandon, D. 1979, 'Zen practice in social work' in D. Brandon and B. Jordan (eds), 1979

Brandon, D. and Jordan, B. (eds) 1979, *Creative Social Work*, Oxford, Blackwell

British Association of Social Workers 1980, 'News: survey shows schools exclude pregnant girls', *Social Work Today*, vol.11, no.32, p.5

Brooks, R. 1980, *Gifted Delinquents*, Brighton Polytechnic (see also *Bright Delinquents*, 1972, NFER)

Bruggen, P. 1979, 'Authority in work with young adolescents', *Journal of Adolescence*, vol.2, no.4, pp.345–54

Cigno, K. 1979, 'In practice', *Community Care*, June 14, pp.14–15

Coleman, J.C. 1980, *The Nature of Adolescence*, London, Methuen

Crompton, M. 1978a, 'Accommodating adolescents', *Community Care*, October 4, p.28

Crompton, M. 1978b, 'Q. When is an adult not an adult? A. When he's an adolescent', *Community Care*, April 12, pp.18–19

Crompton, M. 1980, *Respecting Children: Social Work with Young People*, London, Edward Arnold

Davis, L. 1980, 'The age of consent – is it time for a change in the law?' *Social Work Today*, vol.11, no.19, pp.14–16

Department of Health and Social Security 1974, *Memorandum of Guidance May 1974 HSc(IS) 732*, London, HMSO

Dinnage, R. 1978, 'Social work in a school setting', *Social Work Today*, vol.10, no.2, pp.12–14

Dobson, D. 1979, 'Future developments' in E. Leggett (ed), 1979

Eisenklam, E. 1978, 'Young girls alone in London', *Social Work Today*, vol.10, no.7, pp.23–5

Gaskell, E. 1969, (1864–6), *Wives and Daughters*, Harmondsworth, Penguin Books

Glasser, W. 1975, *Reality Therapy: a New Approach to Psychiatry*, New York and London, Perennial Library, Harper & Row

Goldacre, P. 1979, 'In practice', *Community Care*, April 5, p.11

Grunsell, A. and R., Gurney, P., Josephy, A. and Selway, D. ND., *The Intermediate Centre: The Third Year Report*, London, 6 Cromartie Road, Hornsey N19 3SJ

Grunsell, R. ND., 'The fear of authority', in Grunsell, A. *et al.*, op. cit.

Gutridge, P. 1970, 'The group', *The Forum*, Dr Barnardo's, Autumn issue, pp.120–24

Hadfield, J.A. 1962, *Childhood and adolescence*, Harmondsworth, Penguin Books

Hall, R. 1979, 'An experience of residential life', in D. Brandon and B. Jordan (eds), op. cit.

Harbridge, E. 1981, 'The loneliness of incest', *Community Care*, April 2, pp.12–14

Harris, D. 1979, 'In residence: have a good trip', *Social Work Today*, vol.10, no.18, p.22

Hart, T. 1979, 'Hartfelt', *Community Care*, March 8, p.11

HMSO 1948, *Children Act*

HMSO 1969, *Children and Young Persons Act*

HMSO 1975, *Children Act*

HMSO 1980, *Child Care Act*

Hill, L. 1979, 'Youth information/counselling project', in E. Leggett (ed), op. cit.

Hill, L. 1980, 'Counselling in Wandsworth', *Working with Adolescents*, Leicester, National Youth Bureau, 17–23 Albion Street, LE1 6GD

Hofmann, A.D., Becker, R.D. and Gabriel, H.P. 1976, *The Hospitalized Adolescent*, New York, The Free Press, London, Collier-Macmillan Publications

Hoghughi, M. 1978, *Troubled and Troublesome*, London, Burnett Books/André Deutsch

Hope, P. 1981, 'The empty voice of Youth Call', *Community Care*, June 4, pp.20–21

Howarth, R. and Summers, J. 1978, 'Personal view – children and their welfare', *Social Work Today*, vol.10, no.3, p.19

Howells, J. 1978, 'In residence: balance of power', *Social Work Today*, vol.10, no.2, p.20

Hudson, J. 1978, 'In residence: "They just don't want to know" ', *Social Work Today*, vol.9, no.38, p.23

Hugman, B. 1977, *Act Natural: A New Sensibility for the Professional Helper*, London, Bedford Square Press, National Council of Social Services

Irwin, E.M. 1978, *Growing Pains: A Study of Teenage Distress*, London, The Woburn Press

Jackie, London, D.C. Thompson, October 20 1979

James, G. 1979, 'The child-centred approach to children in care', in D. Brandon and B. Jordan (eds), op. cit.

Jordan, B. 1979, *Helping in Social Work*, London, Routledge & Kegan Paul

Jordan, W. (Bill), 1970, *Client–worker Transactions*, London, Library of Social Work, Routledge & Kegan Paul

Kahan, B. 1981, 'News: eighties should be the quality decade', *Social Work Today*, vol.12, no.32, p.13

Klein, J. 1973, 'Training for the new helping professions – community and youth work', *Occasional papers in community and youth work, no. 1*, University of London, Goldsmiths College

Leeding, A.E. 1976, *Child Care Manual for Social Workers*, 3rd ed, London, Butterworths

Leggett, E. (editor and contributor) 1979, *Wandsworth. A Multi-dis-ciplinary Approach to Intermediate Treatment*, Leicester, National Youth Bureau, 17–23 Albion Street, LE1 6GD

Liebmann, M. 1980, 'Social work in action: contracting into an ordered lifestyle', *Social Work Today*, vol.11, no.30, pp.16–17

Lowe, G.R. 1972, *The Growth of Personality: From Infancy to Old Age*, Harmondsworth, Penguin Books.

McKeever, P. 1979, 'Day-care at Hambro House', in E. Leggett (ed), op. cit.

Merrill, E. 1978, 'Problems of children stuck on glue', *Community Care*, July 12, pp.16–18

Morris, A., Giller, H., Szwed, E. and Geach, H. 1980, *Justice for Children*, Basingstoke, Macmillan

Mortimore, P. 1980, 'Misbehaviour in schools', in G. Upton and A. Gobell (eds), op. cit.

Munro, A. 1978, in E.M. Irwin, op. cit.

Musgrove, F. 1964, *Youth and the Social Order*, London, Routledge & Kegan Paul

National Council for Civil Liberties, ND, *Children have Rights, no. 1, Children in Schools*, 21 Tabard St, London SE1 4LA

National Council for Civil Liberties, ND, *Children have Rights, no. 4, Children at Home*

National Youth Bureau, 1980, *Working with Adoelscents*, Leicester

Nelson, J. and Seddon, J. 1979, 'Children in homes: their opinions, our response', *Child Care Study Papers, no. 3*. London, Church of England Children's Society, Old Town Hall, Kennington Road, SE11 4QD

Northorpe Hall Trust, 1978, *Annual Report* quoted in M. Crompton, 1980, op. cit.

O'Brian, C. 1979, 'In practice', *Community Care*, November 15, p.17

Page, R. and Clark, G.A. (eds), 1977, *Who Cares? Young People in Care Speak Out*, London, National Children's Bureau

Parker, D., Casburn, M. and Turnbull, D. 1981, *Reviewing Juvenile Justice: Adolescents and State Care and Control*, Oxford, Blackwell

Parry, M. 1980. 'Social work in action: Sheila . . . aged 15 . . . violent . . . wants to be loved', *Social Work Today*, vol.11, no.26, pp.18–20

Pearson, G. 1978, 'Social work and law-and-order', *Social Work Today*, vol.9, no.30, pp.18–24

Pidduck, R. 1981, 'Remember the 8th commandment', *Community Care*, January 15, pp.16–18

Porteous, M.A. and Colston, N.J. 1980, 'How adolescents are reported in the British press', *Journal of Adolescence*, vol.3, no.3, pp.197–207

Rae, M., Hewitt, P. and Hugill, B. 1979, 1981, *First Rights. A Guide to Legal Rights for Young People*, National Council for Civil Liberties, 21 Tabard St, London SE1 4LA

Rayman, M. 1979, ' "My stigma – a care order" ',*Community Care*, November 1, pp.21–2

Rayner, E. 1971, *Human Development: An Introduction to the Psycho-dynamics of Growth, Maturity and Ageing*, London, National Institute Social Services Library, Allen & Unwin

Reynolds, D. 1980, 'Employing the young disabled', *Community Care*, August 21, pp.20–22

Robinson, M. 1981, 'Books: missing vitality', *Community Care*, February 19, p.21

Sevenoaks News, February 5 1970, in National Council for Civil Liberties, ND, *Children have rights, no. 1*, London

Stevenson, J. 1979, 'Social work in action: "They never call you by your name in that place" ', *Social Work Today*, vol.11, no.16, pp.18–19

Taylor, L., Lacey, R. and Bracken, D., 1980, *In Whose Best Interests? The Unjust Treatment of Children in Courts and Institutions*, London, The Cobden Trust/Mind (National Association for Mental Health)

Upton, G. and Gobell, A. (eds), 1980, *Behaviour Problems in the Comprehensive School*, University College, Cardiff, Faculty of Education

Wendelken, C. 1981, 'The search for identity', *Social Work Today*, vol.12, no.19, pp.8–10

West, D. 1979, 'The social casework interview', *Social Work Today*, vol.10, no.18, pp.20–21

Willans, A. 1977, *Breakaway: Family Conflict and the Teenage Girl*, London, Temple Smith

Wilson, D. 1981, *Life with a tube*, unpublished

Wilson, P. and Bottomley, V, 1980, 'The emotional climate in the classroom: the interaction between adult teachers and early adolescent studies', in G. Upton and A. Gobell (eds), op. cit.

Winnicott, D.W. 1965, 'Adolescence: struggling through the doldrums', in *The Family and Individual Development*, London, Tavistock Publications, pp.79–87

Wolmar, C. 1980, 'Out in the world – but who cares?' *Community Care*, March 27, pp.20–21

Author Index

Some of the young people who contributed, either directly to the author or through the writing of other authors, appear on more than one page.

Some adults contributed in writing or orally directly to the author and do not appear in the Author Index. Those who are named in the text appear below.

General Index

inadequate, 9, 40, 41, 42, 44
incest, 30, 31, 43, 49
independence, 16, 20, 21, 23, 25,
 35, 63
individual, 13, 17, 19, 21, 31, 32,
 53, 54, 61, 65, 69, 74
intercourse (sexual), 7, 21,29, 30,
 33, 45
interview, 55, 73

journalist, 19
juvenile court, 27, 78

Kneesworth Hall, 37
Korczak, J., 36

label, 13, 20, 52, 53, 57
law, 3, 5, 19, 21, 27, 29, 30, 52, 53,
 60
 legal, 21, 27, 29, 30, 49, 78
 legislation, 26
 illegal, 30
 unlawful, 30, 45
laziness, 52, 53
lecturer, 16
listen, 2, 5, 9, 12, 67, 68
loneliness, 32, 45
love, 2, 3, 4, 6, 7, 13, 15, 32, 33, 48,
 49, 54, 56, 57, 58, 61, 62, 64,
 65, 66, 75,78
 unloveable, 32

maladjusted, 7, 42, 68
marry, 1, 20, 21, 25,29, 33, 48, 49
 marital problems, 28
 matrimonial court, 78
 remarry, 79
masturbation, 23
menarche, 22
money, 6, 21,26, 40, 41, 70, 80
 Section 20 money, 26
moral, 43,44, 48, 52, 74
 immorality, 43
mother, 7, 10, 11, 13, 20, 23, 28, 30,
 38, 42, 44, 48, 54, 63, 73
 mummy, 10, 11
 grandmother, 20

newspaper, 15
nocturnal emission, 23

Northorpe Hall Trust, 65
nurse, 21, 26
 nursery, 24
 nursing staff, 45

offence, 23, 27, 28, 65, 67
 offenders, 27, 77
order,78
 care order, 35, 50, 78
 court order, 49
 probation order, 78
 supervision order, 78

pain, 1, 2, 22, 23, 34, 41, 48, 51, 53,
 55, 59, 65
parent, 1, 7, 8, 10, 11, 17, 19, 21,
 22, 23, 25, 26, 28, 30, 31, 32,
 34, 37, 47, 50, 52, 55, 59, 63,
 67, 75, 78, 79
 parental responsibility, 78
 foster parent, 25
 house parent, 73
peace, 2, 11, 31, 75
period (menstruation), 22
plan, 2, 36, 76, 78, 79
play, 5, 12, 31, 42
Poland, 36
police, 5, 9, 27, 37, 38, 44, 51, 54,
 63, 67, 68, 70, 78
pregnant, 10, 30, 48
 pregnancy, 11, 30, 31, 45, 64, 74
privacy, 55, 74
probation, 57, 59, 73
 detached probation officer, 32,
 56
 Gloucestershire Probation and
 After-Care Committee, 77
 probation officer, 8, 63, 64, 73,
 74
 probation work, 27
psychiatrist, 10, 11, 12, 50, 60, 73
 psychiatric problems, 60
 psychiatric social work, 59
 adolescent psychiatric nit, 52
 Association for the Psychiatric
 Study of Adolescents, 35
 child psychiatric unit, 10, 52
psychologist, 10, 43
 psychololgical, 17, 33
 psycho-pathology, 46